I BELIEVE BECAUSE . . . .

I BELIEVE BECAUSE...

A Study of the Evidence Supporting Christian Faith

Batsell Barrett Baxter

Baker Book House   Grand Rapids, Michigan

ISBN: 0-8010-0548-5
Library of Congress Card Catalog Number: 75-172297

To

My Three Sons

Scott   Alan   John

Foreword

A few weeks ago in a quiet corner of a crowded restaurant I sat across the table from a keen-minded young graduate student of one of our famous American universities. He had been my own student in earlier years, a young man of unusual talent. His keenness of mind, impressive personality, and ability to communicate had marked him for a leader, both in college and in the church. Then came graduate school.

In four short years his whole life had turned around. Now, no longer was there faith in a personal God and, hence, no prayer. Christ was no longer the Saviour and the Bible was just another book. Purpose in life had given way to disillusionment, bordering on despair. Graduation was only a few days away.

Mutual respect still formed a bond between us. Sympathetically I asked, "What will you do now?" The answer was, "I don't know." We talked of the possibility of his teaching, but he said, "I really have nothing that I want to teach." Perhaps some kind of social work, we thought, might be a possibility. He had tried that, working at a government job in a ghetto, "But," he said, "it all seems so futile. I leave the people with just about as many problems as they had before."

There was a pause and then I asked, "What do you see for the future?" A longer pause followed and then the reply, "Nothing." There was a still longer pause as we both thought of the implications of that word *nothing*. Then I asked, "Why

7

have you not ended it all?" Slowly, as the bare area on his cheek, just above the beard, twitched a bit, he replied, "I have thought of that many times." I spoke of my own faith and how that it gave meaning and purpose to my life and expressed the hope that he might again have the faith which he had had in earlier years. He promised to consider it. Our time together was at an end. We walked out into the street, shook hands, and went our separate ways.

What a difference faith in God would make in this young life. With Christ to inspire and to strengthen, what spiritual strength would flow into this young man. With Christian goals and motivation, what heights this life could reach. Somehow as I think back to this conversation I feel that what is true in this young man's life is, in a sense, true of modern twentieth-century civilization. Something has gone wrong. There is something extremely important missing.

Just here a story told by Plutarch of the long ago comes to mind. Two friends received word that a mutual friend had died. They rushed to the home and found the friend's body stretched upon a couch as if in sleep. As they looked upon their friend, they observed that every part of the body seemed to be intact. He appeared so lifelike that they could not believe that he was dead. With one on either side, they lifted up their friend's body and urged him to stand. The body crumpled to the floor. A second time they shook him gently and lifted him to his feet. Again the body crumpled to the floor. As they laid him gently again upon the couch one of the men remarked, "There must be something missing inside." In the lives of many people today, the external things all seem to be perfectly in place and functioning properly, yet something supremely important is missing inside. Whether the application is made to an individual or to society in general, as the sacred writer James put it, "the body apart from the spirit is dead . . . " (James 2:26).

My purpose in writing this book is to help those of our generation whose lives are marked by despair to find hope through faith in God and His Son Jesus Christ. Not just in our time, but especially in our time, there are many who have no real life-goals. Their moral and ethical standards are on shaky ground. Their motivation for living is weak. As honest, sincere, thinking beings they are searching for the answers to life's problems. Mistakenly, they have been led to believe that their dedication to truth will no longer let them hold to their religious faith. They are determined to avoid at all costs anything that might appear to be shallow, wishful thinking. My purpose in this book is to point out solid, respectable reasons for our Christian faith. I believe there are solid foundations for our faith, foundations that will stand the tests of this scientific age. It is my conviction that many have "lost their faith" needlessly, simply because they did not know the evidence which solidly supports Christian faith.

Acknowledgments

No claims of originality are made in this work. I have drawn heavily upon the best writings of our own and other generations. I am especially indebted to the following, from whom I have borrowed extensively: J. D. Thomas, in his fine book, *Facts and Faith,* Vol. I; John Clover Monsma, in his two excellent works, *The Evidence of God in an Expanding Universe* and *Behind the Dim Unknown;* John Klotz, in his monumental work, *Genes, Genesis, and Evolution;* J. D. Bales, in his challenging book, *Atheism's Faith and Fruits;* and C. S. Lewis, in his remarkable books, *The Case for Christianity,* and *Miracles.* Although specific credit is given in each place for the materials used, I feel a special desire to acknowledge my indebtedness to these men. To the many others, from whom I have drawn ideas and information either consciously or unconsciously, I wish to express my appreciation. Throughout the book, whenever Scripture is quoted, I have used the American Standard Version, with an occasional exception where the translation used is identified.

Finally, this book is sent forth with the prayer that it may be of help to many people and that ultimately it may be to the honor and glory of God.

Batsell Barrett Baxter

Contents

Part Four
THE INSPIRATION OF THE BIBLE

Part Five
MIRACLES

Part Six
THE DIVINITY OF CHRIST

Part Seven
SITUATION ETHICS

Part Eight
CONCLUSION

Part One

Introduction

1

Questions Needing Answers

A few years ago the members of a typical Christian family were enjoying a Sunday dinner together when the subject of evolution was mentioned. The father, for no special reason, asked his ten-year-old son if he knew the meaning of the theory of evolution. To his surprise, the boy answered without hesitation, "It is the idea that the world got started by the collecting of lots of cosmic dust. A long time passed, and somehow life began and has developed on up till now." This may not be a very sophisticated explanation of the "big-bang cosmic dust" theory of the origin of the earth, but it indicates quite clearly the effect which television, school textbooks, encyclopedias, and other sources are having upon the minds of young children. This particular ten-year-old boy had been taught from early infancy about the existence of God and the creation of the universe by God's power. At the tender age of ten he saw no special problem in these two divergent explanations of how the earth came into being. That would come later.

Many young people, reared in Christian homes, have accepted the Biblical account of creation and the Christian religion in general without any serious examination of their claims. They have merely accepted these teachings without any real understanding of why they believed these and other important tenets of the Christian faith. Some of these young people at a later time, perhaps while away in military service, or attending a university, or working in the city, have found their childhood faith seriously challenged. Many questions have been asked to which they have known no answers. Many a young person has come home sometime later to announce that he has "lost his faith." One young man, several years along in his pre-medical training, said to his longtime friend, the preacher of the home congregation, "I just don't think that I believe any more." Such a person can become an easy prey to those who would destroy faith. He needs to know the evidence upon which his faith rests. Lest one be open to the charge that his religion is "merely inherited," he should know the evidence upon which his faith is grounded.

In recent generations those who reject Christianity have been more outspoken than ever before. Attacks upon the Christian religion are not new, of course, but they are more widespread and are presented more openly than ever before. Just over a hundred years ago Robert Ingersoll, the noted American orator, went about the land delivering his blasphemous message, "The Mistakes of Moses." Today his message would be considered neither shocking nor blasphemous, for his thesis is essentially the view of many liberal theologians. The "God-is-dead" movement, for example, was not advanced by avowed enemies of the Christian religion, but rather by professors in various liberal theological seminaries. Also, there are many outside the seminaries who are exercising their negative influence in a variety of ways in what might be called a world-wide attack on orthodox Christian faith. Therefore, there is a special need in the twentieth century for each one who believes in God and in the Christian religion to "know whereof he speaks." Many young people are being swept away from the faith, needlessly, because they are not acquainted with the evidence which solidly supports their faith.

A Questioning Age

There was a time when young people generally were quite willing to accept the statements of their parents and religious leaders concerning matters of faith. If there were doubts, they were generally short-lived, and seldom openly expressed. A clear-cut, dogmatic pronouncement from some respected authority was enough to settle the question. It is an understatement to say that that day is gone. The scientific age has brought with it a climate of inquiry. Nothing is too sacred for careful scrutiny. No statement is beyond questioning. It is especially during the high school and college years that young people find themselves examining everything that they have been taught to determine whether or not it is worthy of acceptance. No person, no principle, no institution is exempt from a thorough examination. It is for this reason that young people deserve help in examining the claims of the Christian religion during the questioning period of their lives. Parents likewise need guidance in order that they may be ready to answer the questions which their children are asking.

Actually, the questioning spirit of our age is a healthy sign, for in the long run it should mean a firmer and more vital faith. However, it does place much heavier requirements upon parents, teachers, and religious leaders generally. If the Christian religion is true, it will stand whatever tests are placed upon it. It was Jesus who said, "Ye shall know the truth, and the truth shall make you free" (John 8:32). The apostle Paul wrote to the Thessalonians, "Prove all things; hold fast that which is good" (I Thess. 5:21). Any religion which will not stand careful scrutiny will not long endure, nor should it long endure. We confidently believe that the Christian faith will not only survive but will even prosper under honest, open-minded inquiry.

Among the questions which are being asked by both young and old in this age of inquiry are these:

(1) How did our universe originate?

(2) How old is the earth?

(3) Where did life come from?

(4) Is there a personal God?

(5) Is the God who designed the universe the God of the Bible?

(6) If God created the world, where did evil come from?

(7) If God is good and if God is all-powerful, why does he allow the innocent to suffer?

(8) Is man different from the animals in degree or in kind?

(9) Is the explanation of the creation in Genesis compatible with the theory of evolution?

(10) Is the Bible inspired?

(11) Is truth relative?

(12) Is Jesus of Nazareth the divine Son of God?

(13) Did Jesus really rise from the dead?

(14) Did Jesus ascend into heaven in bodily form?

(15) Is it reasonable to believe in miracles?

(16) Does situation ethics have any validity?

(17) Is the Christian religion likely to decline and die?

(18) Who am I?

(19) What is my destiny?

(20) Is there a literal heaven, and is there a literal hell?

While there are variations of these questions and while there are many other similar questions, these will suffice for the moment. When a question of this magnitude is asked, a parent or teacher might be tempted to say, "Don't ask such things. You must not allow such questions to come into your mind." Such an answer is worse than no answer at all. These are legitimate questions and there are meaningful answers. The purpose of this book is to set forth at least some of these answers.

Christian Evidences

Ours is an age in which the study of the evidences which support the Christian religion is imperative. *"Christian Evidences,"* wrote Leander Keyser some years ago, *"is the scientific proof of the divine authority of the Christian religion."*[1]

---

1. *A System of Christian Evidence,* 10th ed. rev. (Burlington, Iowa: The Lutheran Literary Board, 1953), p. 21.

Evidence is defined as "ground for belief; that which tends to prove or disprove something; . . . data presented to a court or jury in proof of the facts in issue and which may include the testimony of witnesses, records, documents, or objects."[2] Therefore, Christian evidences would be that which is submitted to prove the truth of the Christian religion.

In a relatively recent book, Bernard Ramm has further defined and explained this whole area of study:

> Christian evidences is a discipline within the boundaries of the Christian religion. Christian theology is the Christian religion adequately stated, systematically interrelated, and appropriately defended. It works with the data provided by exegetical theology on the one hand and philosophy on the other. Christian theology assumes the truthfulness of the Christian religion. . . . If it is the function of Christian theology to construct the Christian system, it is the function of Christian apologetics to verify it. . . .
>
> Christian evidences is a subdivision of Christian apologetics. Christian apologetics is the comprehensive, philosophical, theological, and factual demonstration of the truthfulness of our Christian religion. Christian evidences . . . is especially concerned with the demonstration of the *factuality* of the Christian religion.[3]

In exploring the chief areas of Christian faith many questions are regularly asked. It will be the purpose of this book to provide some of the evidences which support Christian faith in the following six major areas of concern: (1) The Existence of God, (2) How the Universe Began, (3) The Inspiration of the Bible, (4) Miracles, (5) The Divinity of Christ, and (6) Situation Ethics.

---

2. *The Random House Dictionary of the English Language* (New York, 1966), p. 495.

3. *Protestant Christian Evidences* by Bernard Ramm. (Chicago: Moody Press, 1933), p. 13. Used with permission of Moody Bible Institute of Chicago.

2

Preliminary Considerations

Near the beginning of this book it seems right and proper to give an explanation of the stand taken by the author. In some areas of study and investigation it is possible for a writer to present various possible hypotheses and then leave the reader to choose from among them that which he believes to be the most dependable. In some cases the author simply provides whatever information he is capable of providing but takes no personal stand. However, considering the matters discussed in this volume, such a position of suspended judgment seems neither praiseworthy nor possible. The very nature of the subjects being discussed makes it imperative that every mature mind draw some conclusions. Life cannot be lived in a state of suspended animation. When one must make moral and ethical decisions daily and almost hourly it is literally impossible not to take a stand on such fundamental issues as the existence of God, the rightness or wrongness of certain behavior, and the like. When a crisis comes in one's life, he either prays to God or he does not. He cannot remain suspended between the two positions.

There is another reason why I feel inclined to take a clear-cut stand on the issues to be discussed in this book. For more than half a century I have been a careful student on all of these issues. I have read extensively, traveled widely, and become acquainted with some of the world's most outstanding thinkers. I now find myself in the position of guide—especially to young people, but also to many others—through the opportunities of pulpit, radio and television. I would be less than responsible were I not to exercise whatever influence I can for the acceptance of those conclusions which I believe to be most valid. Anything less would be both irresponsible and cowardly. My present convictions are based upon careful thought and study over a period of years. The positions which are taken seem more defensible and more logical than any alternate positions.

Having said this, I must also say that it is my intention to keep my mind open to any new evidence that may be forthcoming from any source whatever. The necessity to act requires that a stand be taken. It is also necessary, when one is loyal to his dedication to truth, to be open-minded enough to examine any new evidence which is presented from any source at any time on any subject. To do less is to be afraid of one's position, and to deny a real dedication to the search for the truth. Neither of these positions do I wish to embrace.

Most of us are quite familiar with the scales of justice which are made up of a cross beam to which are attached two pans with the possibility of either pan being weighted more heavily than the other. Such a scale is a device for comparing the relative weights of different objects. With this simple illustration, I believe that it is possible to demonstrate that the side of faith is the heavier of the two sides on each of the major issues to be discussed in this book. I also believe that this is all that can justly be required. Either there is a God or there is not. There can be no in-between. If the evidence supporting the idea of the existence of God is more convincing than the evidence that raises questions and problems about his existence, then the fair-minded reasoner must decide for faith in God. All that is required is that faith be demonstrated to be more reasonable than non-faith.

L. S. Keyser once wrote, "Let us remember this fact: Human reason cannot *prove* the Christian religion to be true. It can only show it to be *more reasonable than unbelief.*"[1]

---

1. *A System of Christian Evidence*, pp. 31-32.

Many years earlier Harvey Everest had written, "We cannot believe unless belief is more rational than unbelief. We cannot believe at will, arbitrarily, or against reason. Reason, meaning thereby the whole mental power for the ascertainment of truth, must be our guide. No one insists upon this more earnestly than the defender of Christianity. Reason and faith are not antagonistic, but rather coadjutors. No faith is worthy unless it is justified by the severest use of reason."[2]

It seems appropriate at this point to state the fundamental thesis of this book: *"There is an infinite, all-wise, all-powerful, all-loving God who has revealed Himself by means natural and supernatural in creation, in the nature of man, in the history of Israel and the Church, in the pages of Holy Scripture, in the incarnation of God in Christ, and in the heart of the believer by the gospel."*[3] It shall be our purpose to demonstrate the reasonableness of the various facets of this position. This is our stand.

Preliminary Observations

In a world such as ours it is obvious that each of us must at times take what may be called the "leap of faith"[4] in connection with our convictions. We do this without embarrassment, for we know that almost every aspect of life requires this same kind of leap of faith. For example, there is a great amount of faith involved in beginning the long, tedious, burdensome program of education. No freshman can possibly know that he will ultimately be successful in finishing high school or college. He begins the long series of studies by faith.

Eating at a restaurant requires faith, for it is quite possible

---

2. *The Divine Demonstration* (St. Louis: Christian Publishing Co., 1884), p. 13.

3. Bernard Ramm, *Protestant Christian Evidences*, p. 33.

4. This is not the "leap of faith" of Kierkegaard and the existentialists, by which they mean a turning away from logical reason to the non-rational approach. Rather, the meaning here is to go as far as one can on reason and the rest of the way on faith.

that in some unnoticed way the food may have become contaminated and therefore be dangerous to one's health. Having a prescription filled at a drugstore likewise requires a certain amount of trust. Similarly, driving a car along a modern highway, riding in an airplane, or even walking along a street requires a certain amount of faith. In still a different way reading a newspaper requires faith. Buying a house, or entering into marriage, or any other major decision of life also involves great faith. So, in religion, too, it is reasonable to expect some necessity of faith. Religion certainly does not stand alone in this regard.

We might also do well to observe that absolute, dogmatic, unequivocal evidence is often not possible in a given situation. However, it is often possible in such situations to demonstrate a strong presumption of truth. There are some situations, by their very nature, which make it impossible to line up all of the evidence on one side of a question. Few things are one hundred percent versus zero percent. In long years of observing and judging college debates, there was never a time when I felt that one team had one hundred percent of the merits and the other team had zero percent. Always it was a matter of sixty—forty, or fifty-five—forty-five, or seventy—thirty, or some other similar balance. In studying the issues it will seldom be possible to show all of the evidence on either side of a question, but we believe that the heavier side of the evidence can be shown to be on the side of Christian faith.

For many years it has been my observation that the entire burden of proof is often forced upon those who believe the Christian religion by those who question it. Often the atheist or agnostic does not shoulder his share of the burden of proof. He asks a barrage of questions, but does not prove his own position. It is easy to ask questions. It is much harder to demonstrate evidence. Let us begin our study by requiring the positions of faith and non-faith to accept equal responsibility to produce evidence.

We note further that proof takes place in the mind—and

the mind may be closed. Evidence does not necessarily prove. It constitutes proof only when the mind is open and honestly considers the evidence. Perhaps you are familiar with the story of the two boys who had a contest to see which one could scare the largest number of rats out from under the barn. The first boy placed his friend on the opposite side of the barn, took a long pole and rattled it loudly beneath the barn. Rats scattered in every direction. The first boy called to his friend, "Did you see any rats?" The answer came back, "No, not one." How was that possible? There had been more rats running in every direction than one could count, visible to anyone who would look. The first boy went around the barn to see why his friend had seen no rats, only to find him with his eyes tightly closed. He had seen no rats, not because there were no rats to see, but because his eyes were closed. Sometimes the evidence for the Christian religion is ineffective because the mind has been closed.

Homer Hailey pointed out that the acceptance of evidence depends upon five things:

(1) The weight of the evidence.

(2) The clarity with which the evidence is presented.

(3) The honesty of the examiner of the evidence, i.e., the hearer.

(4) The logical ability of the hearer to evaluate evidence.

(5) The background prejudices of the hearer.[5]

In our study we shall not settle all problems nor answer all questions, but we confidently believe that we shall be able to settle and answer many. We believe that we shall leave the field of discussion with fewer problems and questions than those who deny the existence of God and His creation of the universe. All that we ask is an open, fair examination of the evidence.

In the preliminary analysis of this whole field of study it is also well for us to distinguish between the words *hypothesis,*

5. *Evidences Quarterly,* IV, 1 (1964), 4.

theory, and *fact* (or law). An hypothesis is a preliminary idea about how something may function. It is an intelligent guess, not yet supported by significant evidence. Theory, on the other hand, is an hypothesis which has progressed to a higher stage by reason of some meaningful evidence. It has not yet been demonstrated in the full, absolute sense, but there is some supporting evidence to cause it to be given greater credence than the original hypothesis. Then, there is fact, or law. This is a theory that has been demonstrated over and over again, and has therefore been accepted generally as a basic law of nature. It is capable of verification by competent scientists.

There are other preliminary observations. For example, sometimes people who have taken something for granted without question are disturbed when they are introduced to problems concerning what they have previously believed. As one example, we might mention the age of the earth. There are some who have so long believed certain explanations that they find any divergent evidence disturbing. It is our conviction that in the long run it is better to face the problem, find the evidence, and then know the truth concerning the matter. To remain in ignorance, even though one may be fully satisfied in one's ignorance, is hardly a defensible position. We ought to be ready for any truth that can actually be demonstrated to be truth.

Finally, it must be pointed out that when a young person faces a question for which he does not know an answer, he is likely to feel that there is no answer. Not knowing the answer, he concludes that no one knows an answer, or that there is no answer. This has led many a young person to abandon various aspects of his religious faith, unnecessarily. If he had been better informed, he would not have been overwhelmed by some problem or question. It does not necessarily follow that when a young person does not know the answer to a question, there is no answer.

Scope of Christian Evidences

The scope of Christian evidences is, as pointed out by Bernard Ramm:

> . . . .*that of demonstrating that Christianity is the religion which pertains to reality by reason of its factuality.* . . . the focus is upon the *factuality* . . . . By *fact* we mean either some objective *thing* (as an archaeological dig or artifact), or some *event* (as a historical battle), or some *phenomenon* which may be personal (as in the case of Paul's conversion), or *social* (as in the spread of the Christian Church). These *facts* may be classified three ways. . . . First, there is *material fact*. By *material fact* we refer to anything of a very concrete, specific nature, e.g., things, historical events, meteorological phenomena, documents, or monuments. Secondly, there is *supernatural fact,* which involves *events* or *phenomena* which can only be satisfactorily accounted for by invoking the category of the supernatural. Thirdly, there is *experiential fact* which refers to the experiences of people, and social phenomena which are traceable back to the impact of the Christian religion.[6]

This is a rather concrete statement of the areas in which we may expect to find evidence to use in our discussions of the various facets of the Christian faith.

Robert Morris Page has pointed out some of our limitations in making observations. In reasoning concerning such matters as the existence of God, we must recognize our own limited perspective. For example, when ships were built of wood everyone would have considered it ridiculous to think that iron could float. A blacksmith would immediately demonstrate the impossibility of iron floating by putting a horseshoe in a tub of water and watching it sink. However, if he had only had the insight to do so he could have demonstrated the truthfulness of the opposite by putting a wash

6. Ramm, pp. 16-17.

basin into his tub of water, thus anticipating the eventual discovery that iron ships could float.[7]

Page then pointed out, "Sometimes a full test of a hypothesis requires observations that are not available to a particular observer. For example, suppose an observer is limited in his observation to the surface of the ocean. This observer can see nothing that is above or below the surface of the water. . . ."[8] Page added that while the observer is aware of boats and other things floating in the water, he knows nothing at all about submarines and fish swimming below the water or about birds and airplanes flying above the water. Think how incredible it would be to him to hear the testimony of someone who could observe above and beneath the water. His own limited perspective would make such information seem unbelievable. Since our powers of observation are limited to a relatively small portion of all reality we must be slow to question such things as the existence of God.

With open minds, we are now ready to examine evidence of whatever kind and from whatever source as it relates to the idea of God and the universe. With some awareness of our own limited perspective and of man's tendency to see what he wants to see we set out on our search for truth cautiously and humbly. Yet, guided by the principles of logical reasoning, and with an awareness of the methods of modern science, we set out with the high hope of discovering truth.

---

7. "A Conclusive Test," *The Evidence of God in an Expanding Universe,* ed. John Clover Monsma (New York: G. P. Putnam's Sons, 1958), p. 26.

8. Page, pp. 26-27.

Part Two

The Existence of God

"The greatest question of our time is not communism vs. individualism, nor Europe vs. America, not even the East vs. the West; it is whether men can bear to live without God."

—Will Durant

3

Two Hypotheses

Now that we have certain preliminary considerations in mind, we turn our attention to our first major issue, the existence of God. This is obviously the first significant issue of our study, for if there be no God we need not go any further. It is also the most basic issue, for upon it all of the other issues rest. We begin, then, by bringing all of our faculties, both physical and mental, to bear on the simple question of whether or not there is a God. The Biblical view is that God is an eternal Being who is omnipotent, omniscient, omnipresent, holy, just, and merciful. He is not only the first Cause but the Being who maintains and supervises the universe. Unless we can be convinced that there is a God, it is pointless to talk about creation, or the inspiration of the Bible, or miracles, or the divinity of Christ. In this chapter and in the several which follow we turn our attention to the evidences which support the idea that there is a God in heaven.

Sometime in the first half of the nineteenth century the noted religious commentator, Adam Clarke, gave this description of God:

A general definition of this great First Cause, as far as human words dare attempt one, may be thus given: The eternal, independent, and self-existent Being; the Being whose purposes and actions spring from himself, without foreign motive or influence: he who is absolute in dominion; the most pure, the most simple, the most spiritual of all essences; infinitely benevolent, beneficent, true, and holy: the cause of all being, the upholder of all things; infinitely happy, because infinitely perfect; and eternally self-sufficient, needing nothing that he has made: illimitable in his immensity, inconceivable in his mode of existence, and indescribable in his essence; known fully only to himself, because an infinite mind can be fully apprehended only by itself. In a word, a Being who, from his infinite wisdom, cannot err or be deceived; and who, from his infinite goodness, can do nothing but what is eternally just, right, and kind. Reader, such is the God of the Bible; but how widely different from the God of most human creeds and apprehensions![1]

As we begin our study of the existence of God, notice two opposing hypotheses. Remember, an hypothesis is an idea of how things might be, suggested by a preliminary examination of the situation, but not so adequately supported as to become a full-fledged theory, and certainly not yet a demonstrable law.

Wishing God into Existence

Our first hypothesis was suggested by Sigmund Freud, the Vienna psychiatrist who is generally known as the father of psychoanalysis, in his book, *The Future of an Illusion*.[2] He argues that religion is merely the *projection of a wish*. Actually, he says, there is nothing "out there," meaning that there is no God.

Freud believed that man, because of his fears, developed the idea of a protective father. He believed that man created God, rather than that God created man. There were, according to Freud, three chief causes which led man to project the idea of a protective, heavenly father. First, man fears the unpredictability, the impersonality, and the ruthlessness of nature, which often rides roughshod over him. Freud was thinking of such things as famines, diseases, earthquakes, and the like. A specific example might be a South Sea Island

---

1. *Commentary* (New York: Abingdon-Cokesbury Press, n.d.), I, 27.
2. Trans. W. D. Robson-Scott (New York: Liveright Publishing Corp., 1953).

native, who hears rumblings within the earth and sees an extinct volcano give signs of renewed life. Unable to flee from the island, unable to quench the fire of the volcano, and unable to dam back its molten lava, he falls down and prays to some superhuman being, asking him to protect his family, his possessions, and himself. According to Freud, these great, powerful, destructive forces of nature cause man to wish for an agency, a power, a being who could control them.

In the second place, Freud argued that man is afraid because of his relationship to his fellowmen. Men often act unpredictably, brutally, and unjustly to each other. Hence, when man finds himself threatened or endangered by his fellowman, he projects the wish that there be a judge who is big enough and powerful enough to insist that justice be done. Hence, divine law takes form. Righteousness and justice come into being. This is a subtle projection of the wish for the orderliness of things, said Freud. In short, man feels a need for an umpire or referee to protect his rights and to see that justice prevails.

In the third place, Freud argued that man is conscious, more and more as he gets older, that he will disintegrate and die. Man finds it very difficult to accept the idea of complete extinction. The inconclusiveness of existence, the destruction of his hopes, the lack of fulfillment of his dreams, and his own mental and physical decline bear in on him. In most cultures, man tries to eliminate all mention of death, and tries to look and act as young as he can. This fear, said Freud, creates the wish for religion. Here is the concept of the father again, with the return of his children to heaven, where all things will be eternally right.

Freud's arguments are effective. In fact, upon first hearing them, a young person may feel overwhelmed and even conclude that there is no answer to these propositions. However, we must point out that this whole explanation of life is Freudian psychology, merely the Freudian interpretation of the way man thinks about the world. This is an hypothesis and is not actual evidence or proof. This is just one possible hypothesis for explaining the way the world operates and man thinks. In its simplest form, this hypothesis holds that man is weak and inadequate in many situations of life and therefore has wished God into existence, to protect and keep him in safety.

We would ask, "Does the fact that man needs God and wishes for God actually disprove that God exists?" I might, for example, put this hypothesis to the test by saying, "I have three sons who feel a need for a father to provide for their physical needs and to suggest guidelines for the living of their lives. They wish for a father. They feel a need for a father. Therefore, I do not exist, but am merely a product of their wishful thinking." But, the fact is, I do exist. Their needing me and wishing for me causes me neither to exist, nor not to exist. Hence, man's feeling of need for some protection against the ruthlessness of nature, the ruthlessness of his fellowmen, and the disintegration that comes with age and death, proves neither that there is a God nor that there is not a God. It is merely a possible explanation, not yet supported with evidence which constitutes proof.

Wishing God out of Existence

Next, consider an opposite hypothesis: Man wishes God not to exist. I believe I can make a strong case for the idea that modern man really wishes that there were no God. It would go something like this.

Modern man possesses great pride in himself and in his accomplishments. He looks about himself and rejoices in his ability to cross the oceans and the continents. He is master of even the highest mountains and the deepest seas. He can brave the cold of the Antarctic, and the heat of the Sahara. In fractions of a second he can speak around the world and send pictures to the far corners of the earth. He can reach out into space and land on the moon, a sophisticated accomplishment almost beyond the comprehension of most men. Man can transport himself under the earth, on the sea, on land, through the air and even through space with great efficiency and at great speed. He can build great skyscrapers, huge bridges, intricate computers, and countless other machines to do his work for him. He has learned to preserve sound on magnetic tape for future use, just as he has learned to preserve scenes on film for later use.

He can project his own natural abilities such as walking, hearing, seeing, speaking, and the like through mechanical processes. Through the use of advanced medical science he can cure many diseases, substitute organs in the human body for those that are worn out, and in general extend his life span. He can think, remember, invent, and construct. There is almost no limit to what man can do. Therefore, there is a tendency in our twentieth century for man to feel that he is self-sufficient, independent, and without any need for God. Man can care for himself and for his every need. Man's pride leads to self-worship, for man tends to make himself his own god.

Further, in his pride modern man does not wish to be subject to any divine being, nor to the moral, ethical, and religious restrictions which God would place upon him. He seeks freedom from any outside limitations upon his own desires. Consequently, he engages in wishful thinking and eliminates the idea of God. He says, "God is dead." This releases great amounts of time for his own use, since he does not need to worship or work for God. This releases great amounts of money for his own use, since he does not need to give to God or to His causes. This frees him from many moral, ethical, and religious restrictions. Modern man strongly wishes not to believe in God because of what he considers advantages to himself. Perhaps this is only in his subconscious, but it nevertheless serves as the basis for his overt actions in rejecting God and religion in general. This forms the foundation out of which he doubts and disbelieves in the existence of God. Instead of the believer in God being the wishful thinker, as Freud had it, the disbeliever is the wishful thinker.

Evaluation

Perhaps it should immediately be admitted that if we are to argue that Freud's idea is only an hypothesis, the same would have to be said for the idea just stated. This is true. Neither of these hypotheses has been proved with complete, final, demonstrable evidence. I have suggested the latter hypothesis in order to take some of the force out of Freud's presentation, and also to suggest that in determining the truth or falsity of an idea there must be the presentation of real evidence, rather than a cursory, general survey of the situation. Actually, we are just now ready to seek solid evidence for the idea that God exists.

Before leaving the two hypotheses presented in this chapter, however, it should be pointed out that it is extremely difficult to find something that is absolutely certain, for our senses may deceive us. When we think we are producing evidence, we may actually be projecting our own wishes. Certainty is possible, however, though it must be sought with great care. Some of the world's greatest philosophers have demonstrated the difficulty of finding a beginning point that is absolutely and unequivocally true. It was Descarte who, in trying to achieve absolute certainty of some bit of knowledge, eventually came forth with the statement, "I think, therefore, I am." It would be difficult to deny that he had found a beginning point of which he could be absolutely certain. At another time, Descarte was writing in his room on a cold winter day and could feel the heat from a nearby stove. He reasoned that it was not auto-suggestion—not wishful thinking. It was real. He could feel the heat and therefore he knew that there was heat. Similarly, there are some kinds of knowledge that come at us with great force because they are.

In arguing for the superiority of the hypothesis of faith over the hypothesis of atheism, I would remind you that from the time of Adam and Eve, in Genesis 3, man has tried to hide from God because of his sin, but there has been no place to hide. Escape from God is impossible because God is infinite. The psalmist, David, wrote:

Whither shall I go from thy Spirit?
Or whither shall I flee from thy presence?
If I ascend up into heaven, thou art there:
If I make my bed in Sheol, behold, thou art there.
If I take the wings of the morning,
And dwell in the uttermost parts of the sea;
Even there shall thy hand lead me,
And thy right hand shall hold me.
                              —Psalm 139:7-10

Evidently, David also felt this inability to escape from God. It is not as Freud says. Religion is not auto-suggestion, for man has often wanted to run away from God rather than to wish God into existence. Even today, man is still related to God even though he often wishes to escape. It is as Augustine said, "Thou madest us for Thyself, and our heart is restless, until it repose in Thee."[3] It is more likely, or so it seems to me, that modern man will endeavor to escape from God rather than to wish God into existence.

---

3. "The Confessions of Augustine," trans. Edward B. Pusey, *The Harvard Classics,* ed. Charles W. Eliot (New York: F. W. Collier & Son, 1909), VII, 5.

4

Augustine's Intuitional and Anselm's Ontological Arguments

Through the centuries the most eminent thinkers have put forward from time to time arguments that have come to be known as the classical arguments for the existence of God. It is difficult to know who first stated these arguments, since they have been stated and restated by countless men over the long sweep of history. The two men whose names we associate with these formalized arguments for the existence of God discussed in this chapter are men who have given unusually clear and forceful statements of the arguments.

The Argument from Intuition

Augustine, who lived in the fourth and fifth centuries A.D., believed from his own feelings and from his observations that man has a direct intuition of the existence of God. There is something about the way we human beings are made that causes us to know that both we and the universe about us are products of God. This argument finds support in the fact, as borne out by modern anthropologists, that man is incurably religious, whether he be Jew or Gentile, whether he be educated or uneducated, whether he lived in an ancient time or in a modern period. Wherever man has been found, in whatever century and in whatever part of the world, he has been found to be a worshiping creature. This is because of man's sense of finitude in his own nature. According to

Augustine, this is an inevitable consequence of the way the universe and man are made. Man instinctively looks upward to find God.

This argument, while not quite convincing to the modern scientific mind, is quite at home in the twentieth century, a century in which existentialism has found a great deal of respect and support. There are many who do not wish to bother with logical evidence. They prefer to accept what seems right to them. Feelings are more important than empirical evidence, that is, evidence which comes through the physical senses. Whatever is personally satisfying is acceptable. I mention the argument from intuition, not so much because this argument is convincing to the rational mind, but because it ought not to be discounted entirely. By itself it is not enough, but it is deeply significant that down through the centuries wherever men have been found they have exhibited some kind of religious faith and worship.

Looking at another facet of this argument of intuition, we may reason by analogy that if a man who had never seen the modern system of electrical wiring in a home should find an extension cord with a two-pronged plug on the end, he would instinctively know that there must be something, somewhere, specifically designed for the prongs to fit. He would, if he were an intelligent and logical being, begin to look for something akin to a wall socket, into which his new found plug might fit. Similarly, when we find man universally worshiping, we expect to find something worthy of his worship.

Yet another analogy may help to make this argument more meaningful. In Washington, D.C., the most spectacular of our national monuments is to be found. The 550-foot monolithic Washington Monument towers above the entire city. When visitors drive their cars into the monument area, park them at the base of this huge structure, and step out of their cars, instinctively their eyes rise from the base to the top. There is something about the situation that causes visitors instinctively to lift their eyes from the earth upward to the top of the monument. Similarly, there is something about the way

our universe is made and the way man is made that causes
him to lift his eyes to the heavens to seek God.

Dr. Alexis Carrel, one of the world's most famous doctors
and a Nobel prize winner, once wrote:

> Despite its stupendous immensity, the world of matter is
> too narrow for man. Like his economic and social envi-
> ronment, it does not fit him. . . . With the aid of mathe-
> matical abstractions his mind apprehends the electrons as
> well as stars. He is made on the scale of the terrestrial
> mountains, oceans, and rivers. . . . But he also belongs to
> another world. A world which, although enclosed within
> himself, stretches beyond space and time.[1]

This is a different way of stating the same general argument.
There is something about man, although somewhat indefin-
able, that reaches beyond the material universe in which he
finds himself.

Dr. Paul Clarence Aebersold, a biophysicist, quoted
Francis Bacon, the English philosopher and statesman of
more than three centuries ago:

> A little philosophy inclines man to atheism; a depth of
> philosophy brings him into religion. Aebersold added,

Aebersold added,

> Whether by means of intellect or spirit, the fact is that
> man has almost universally recognized a greater all-
> encompassing intelligence and order in the universe than
> could possibly be conceived from chance, haphazard
> events involving inanimate, unguided matter. That man
> universally accepts the need of extrapolation beyond his
> own intellect is in itself strong evidence for a superior
> Intelligence.[2]

Anselm's Ontological Proof

In the late middle ages Anselm introduced to the philosophical and religious worlds a clever philosophical argument

---

1. *Man the Unknown,* 59th ed. (New York: Harper & Brothers, 1938), p. 320.
2. "Physical Evidences of God," *The Evidence of God in an Expanding Universe,* ed. John Clover Monsma, pp. 59-60.

for the existence of God. While it is difficult both to understand and to appreciate, it deserves to be stated and considered. It is generally referred to as the ontological argument since ontology is that branch of philosophy that deals with the nature of being or existence.

Anselm began with a definition, *"God is that than which nothing greater can be conceived!"* Then he argued that man is able to conceive in his mind of the *idea* that than which there is no greater. At this point he introduced the statement, "But I can think of something that is greater than the *idea* of that than which there is no greater." Someone asked, "What?" The answer came: "The *existence* of that than which there is no greater." Hence, by very definition, God must exist. Turn this over in your mind. Does it have validity? Is it a mere conundrum? It is certainly difficult to disprove, yet there is a haunting feeling that it does not say much. Actually, if one grants Anselm's definition, then the argument seems to have validity. However, at best it is a philosophical argument much better suited to another age than our scientific twentieth century.

We are all familiar with the statement in the Psalms, "The fool hath said in his heart, There is no God" (Ps. 14:1). In order for the fool to say "God," he had to have a concept of God in his mind. To start out to deny God is a kind of implication that God exists. This, too, is a part of the ontological approach.

Is it possible to think of something that does not exist? The reader is likely to think that it is easily possible to think of something that does not actually exist, but this is too quick a response. What we are really asking is, "Can you think of something that has never been thought of before, not just some new combination of previously known elements, but something that is absolutely new?" A few years ago the jet plane made its appearance. How would one describe it to someone who had not seen it before? Probably he would do so in terms of a comparison with previous airplanes, such as, "It is larger than the DC-6, having a wider wingspread, more powerful motors, and a greater seating capacity. It is unusual in that its motors have no propellers, but rather push the plane through the air by the force of their exhausts." Actually, you see, the jet plane was like something that had gone before. Most of our teaching is done in terms of comparisons of that which is known with that which is not yet known. It is this principle upon which the ontological argument is based. It concludes that man cannot think, in the absolute sense, of something that does not exist. Therefore, when man thinks of God, it is an argument that God must exist.

The best statement that I have seen concerning this matter appears in a little book called *Philosophy of Religion* by Dr. William H. Davis:

> Let us now express the ontological argument in different terms altogether. Let us conceive of "everything whatever" and classify this "everything" into two groups, namely, those things which exist (now), and those which do not exist. Let us further divide this "everything" as between those things which are impossible, contingent, and necessary.
>
> By "impossible" we mean self-contradictory and unthinkable. Square circles are impossible in this sense. . . . By "contingent" we mean something like "maybe, maybe not." For example, the reader of this book exists, but he exists contingently—that is, he might cease to exist. . . . Whatever can come into being or can go out of being is called contingent. A good synonym for contingent is "dependent." Finally, by "necessary" we mean whatever *has* to exist and cannot not-exist, if there be any such thing. These divisions can be illustrated by the following chart:

NON-EXISTING		EXISTING	
Impossible	Contingent		Necessary
"a"	"b"	"c"	"d"

We may now say where anything we might think of can be located on this chart. Unicorns, for example, fall into section "b." That is, they do not exist, but they *might.* The Washington Monument falls in section "c." That is, it does exist, but might *not.* The question of interest, however, is where God is to be placed on the chart. . . . Thus, by examining what we mean by "God," we see that He does not fit in either section "a," "b," or "c." Thus, He must fit in section "d." Since God is not impossible or contingent, He must be necessary. But whatever is necessary, exists.[3]

Conclusion

While neither the intuitional argument nor the ontological argument would be sufficient to send a thoughtful, questioning mind on its way with absolute confidence that there is a God in heaven, these arguments cannot be dismissed entirely. Actually, they grow on you. The more you think of them, the more you feel that there is something behind each. As we turn now to the more convincing evidences for the existence of God, we leave these two preliminary arguments to mature and ripen in the reader's mind.

3. (Abilene, Texas: Biblical Research Press, 1969), pp. 9-11.

5

The Moral Law Within

In his *Critique of Practical Reason,* Immanuel Kant wrote,
"Two things fill the mind with . . . admiration and awe . . .
the starry heavens above and the moral law within."[1] Kant
was referring to the "uniform universe," which we shall
consider in later chapters, and to the "sense of ought," which
is our concern in this chapter. This "sense of ought," this
moral sense within man, is not merely the result of the mores
or customs of his culture. Rather, it is an innate capacity to
know right and wrong. That man has this capacity can hardly
be explained unless there is a moral governor of the universe.
It implies a moral creator, God. It is universally observed that
human beings try to convince themselves that their actions
are right and justifiable. They desire the approval of their
consciences, as well as the approval of their fellowmen. Is it
unreasonable to assume that the presence of a moral nature
in man is an indication of a moral governor? Why should man
be concerned with the demands of conscience if he is nothing
more than a chance combination of atoms?

This is an aspect of man's nature that makes him unique,
for the other creatures of the earth do not have this inner,
moral sense. For example, an ox has no sense of right and
wrong. If an ox gores a man to death, he is not arrested,
tried, and condemned to the electric chair. Rather, we recognize his inability to make moral judgments, confine him in a

---

1. Trans. Thomas K. Abbott, in *Kant, Great Books of the Western World,* Vol.
42, ed-in-chief [Robert M. Hutchins] (Chicago: Encyclopedia Brittanica, Inc.,
1952), p. 361.

sturdier pen, and warn everyone not to come near him. When a man commits the same crime of killing a man, his treatment is vastly different. The only reason that it is logical for it to be different is that man has an ethical and moral sense of what is right and what is wrong.

We are not speaking, when we speak of the moral law within, of any one system or set of principles. Rather, we are speaking of man's innate capacity to know right from wrong. It is akin to his conscience. This is uniquely a human quality, for animals do not possess it. It is a significant part of what is meant in the Scriptures when we read that man was created in the image of God (Gen. 1:26). This capacity within man is an evidence of the existence of God, for unless there were a moral creator behind him man could not have this unique quality.

This inner sense of right and wrong is referred to from time to time in the Scriptures. For example the apostle Paul recognized it when he wrote, "When Gentiles that have not the law do by nature the things of the law, these, not having the law, are the law unto themselves; in that they show the work of the law written in their hearts, their conscience bearing witness therewith, and their thoughts one with another accusing or else excusing them" (Rom. 2:14-15). Paul seems to be saying that those who never knew of the Law of Moses would not be judged by that law which they had no opportunity to know, but would be judged on the basis of their own sense of right and wrong, the law written in their hearts.

Theoretically, according to this teaching, it is possible for man not to sin. If he lives up perfectly to the best that he has the capability of knowing, he never becomes a sinner and therefore is never lost. However, we hasten to add that it is all but impossible for anyone to live up perfectly even to the most elemental moral and ethical code. Inevitably, he violates his sense of right conduct. When man does this he becomes a sinner and is lost, or estranged, from God. The emphasis of the New Testament is that the only hope of salvation is in

Christ. Only through the love of God, as manifest in Christ, can man be forgiven and saved (John 3:16). Hence, Jesus could say, "I am the way, and the truth, and the life: no one cometh unto the Father, but by me" (John 14:6).

The Law of Human Nature

C. S. Lewis, fellow of Magdalen College of Oxford University until his recent death, was one of the world's most effective apologists for the Christian religion. He had, himself, been an atheist or agnostic in his earlier years, but he eventually came to a solid faith in the existence of God and the validity of the Christian religion. In his book *Mere Christianity* he published a series of radio talks made over the British Broadcasting Company stations in England. In a series of five relatively brief talks he showed in a very meaningful way how the moral law within man is an evidence of the existence of God. The following paragraphs are taken from these radio talks. Lewis presented the moral nature of man as a major argument for the existence of a moral creator behind the universe:

> Every one has heard people quarrelling. Sometimes it sounds funny and sometimes it sounds merely unpleasant; but however it sounds, I believe we can learn something very important from listening to the kind of things they say. They say things like this: "How'd you like it if anyone did the same to you?"—"That's my seat; I was there first."—"Leave him alone; he isn't doing you any harm."—"Why should you shove in first?"—"Give me a bit of your orange. I gave you a bit of mine."—"Come on, you promised." People say things like that every day, educated people as well as uneducated, and children as well as grownups. . . . [Man] is appealing to some kind of standard of behaviour which he expects the other man to know about. . . . Nearly always he tries to make out that what he has been doing does not really go against the standard, or that if it does there is some special excuse. . . . It looks, in fact, very much as if both parties had in mind some kind of Law or Rule of fair play or

decent behaviour or morality or whatever you like to call
it, about which they really agreed. And they have. If they
had not, they might, of course, fight like animals, but
they could not *quarrel* in the human sense of the word.
Quarrelling means trying to show that the other man is in
the wrong. And there would be no sense in trying to do
that unless you and he had some sort of agreement as to
what Right and Wrong are; just as there would be no
sense in saying that a footballer had committed a foul
unless there were some agreement about the rules of
football.

Now this Law or Rule about Right and Wrong used to
be called the law of Nature. . . . they really meant the
Law of *Human* Nature.[2]

Later, Lewis said this:

I know that some people say the idea of a Law of
[Human] Nature or decent behaviour known to all men is
unsound, because different civilisations and different ages
have had quite different moralities.

But this is not true. There have been differences between their moralities, but these have never amounted to
anything like a total difference. If anyone will take the
trouble to compare the moral teaching of, say, the ancient Egyptians, Babylonians, Hindus, Chinese, Greeks
and Romans, what will really strike him will be how very
like they are to each other and to our own. . . . Think of
a country where people were admired for running away in
battle, or where a man felt proud of double-crossing all
the people who had been kindest to him. You might just
as well try to imagine a country where two and two made
five. . . . Selfishness has never been admired. Men have
differed as to whether you should have one wife or four.
But they have always agreed that you must not simply
have any woman you liked. . . .

. . . None of us are really keeping the Law of Nature. . . .

. . . this year, or this month, or, more likely, this very
day, we have failed to practise ourselves the kind of
behaviour we expect from other people. . . . The truth is,

2. From *Mere Christianity* by C. S. Lewis. (New York: The Macmillan
Company, 1943, 1945, 1952), pp. 3-4. Used with permission.

we believe in decency so much—we feel the Rule or Law pressing on us so—that we cannot bear to face the fact that we are breaking it, and consequently we try to shift the responsibility. For you notice that it is only for our bad behaviour that we find all these explanations. It is only our bad temper that we put down to being tired or worried or hungry; we put our good temper down to ourselves.

These, then, are the two points I wanted to make. First, that human beings, all over the earth, have this curious idea that they ought to behave in a certain way, and cannot really get rid of it. Secondly, that they do not in fact behave in that way. . . .[3]

Some objected to Lewis' argument, so he responded in a subsequent radio talk:

Isn't what you call the Moral Law simply our herd instinct and hasn't it been developed just like all our other instincts? . . . We all know what it feels like to be prompted by instinct—by mother love, or sexual instinct, or the instinct for food. . . . But feeling a desire to help is quite different from feeling that you ought to help whether you want to or not.[4]

The illustration Lewis used is of a man who suddenly is faced with an emergency situation. Standing on the bank of a swiftly moving stream, he notices someone in the water about to drown, calling for help. Two instincts or impulses immediately register themselves: (1) the desire to plunge into the water and help save the man's life, and (2) the desire to avoid danger and not to risk one's own life in attempting to rescue another.

Lewis continued:

But you will find inside you, in addition to these two impulses, a third thing which tells you that you ought to follow the impulse to help, and suppress the impulse to run away. Now this thing that judges between two in-

3. Lewis, pp. 5-7.
4. Lewis, p. 8.

stincts, that decides which should be encouraged, cannot itself be either of them. . . . If two instincts are in conflict, and there is nothing in a creature's mind except those two instincts, obviously the stronger of the two must win. But at those moments when we are most conscious of the Moral Law, it usually seems to be telling us to side with the weaker of the two impulses.[5]

Lewis next faced the objection that what he has been calling the Law of Human Nature is merely social convention, something that is put into us by education, and that these social conventions differ from country to country and from civilization to civilization. He responded that while there are differences of customs, there is a hard central area of ethical and moral law that is almost universal. He continued:

The moment you say that one set of moral ideas can be better than another, you are, in fact, measuring them both by a standard, saying that one of them conforms to that standard more nearly than the other. But the standard that measures two things is something different from either. You are, in fact, comparing them both with some Real Morality. . . . The reason why your idea of New York can be truer or less true than mine is that New York is a real place, existing quite apart from what either of us thinks.[6]

Lewis' arguments were designed to demonstrate that if there is a sense of ought within man, there must be some kind of moral or ethical being behind the universe. Man cannot, if he is a moral being, be simply an accidental concourse of atoms. Lewis stated it this way:

We have only got as far as a Somebody or Something behind the Moral Law. We are not taking anything from the Bible or the Churches, we are trying to see what we can find out about this Somebody on our own steam. . . . We have two bits of evidence about the Somebody. One

5. Lewis, pp. 8-9.
6. Lewis, pp. 10-11.

is the universe He has made. . . . The other bit of evidence is that Moral Law which He has put into our minds.[7]

Additional Support

Dr. Henry M. Morris, an engineer, makes the following comment:

> One further conclusion comes easily. There is something in our own finite personalities that we call a conscience or a moral urge. Whatever it is, each individual, however benighted, recognizes something in him that tells him that he ought to do the thing that is right morally and ought to shun the wrong—even though individual standards as to what constitutes right and wrong seem to vary somewhat with time and place. As far as personalities in the universe are concerned, at least, it is a moral universe. Therefore, the Creator is a moral being, who has placed in His creatures a moral consciousness.[8]

Dr. James D. Bales, an educator, holds that the unpredictable nature of man indicates that there is something in man that is not under the laws of mechanical force or matter. It is difficult to make an occasional prediction of the choice that man will make between various alternatives before him, and the choice is not necessarily an unavoidable decision.[9]

Dr. Robert Horton Cameron, a mathematician, argues that man is a creature of choice, which implies that he is not merely a product of mechanistic influences and pressures:

> "Is there a God?" That question implies thought—ability to *think*. I cannot conceive of such ability without an enabling Power. I am not an automaton. . . . Logic can decide whether a mathematical argument is a proof, but thought can create the argument in the first place. It can invent new mathematical concepts and discover new theorems. Thought involves the possibility of self-analysis and self-criticism. A machine can be built to play chess, but it cannot chuckle over an opponent's mistake, or

7. Lewis, p. 23.
8. *Studies in the Bible and Science* (Grand Rapids, Michigan: Baker Book House, 1966), p. 14.
9. *Atheism's Faith and Fruits* (Boston: W. A. Wilde Company, 1951), p. 44.

regret a mistake of its own. Thought involves something that goes beyond a mechanism or mechanical rules. To me it indicates that a mechanistic philosophy is inadequate to explain man or mankind. I can *think!*

I also believe in God because He has given me *emotions.* . . . Our very emotional nature is an evidence of the Creator's wisdom. What would our lives be like without emotions? How long would the race survive without the sex urge and the emotions connected with it? Why is it that infant mortality is lowest when babies are loved?

I believe in God because he has given me *moral judgment.* The race has an innate sense of right and wrong. . . . My belief in God is also based on intelligent volition—on the human *will,* which has been explained as "the total conscious process involved in effecting a decision." *Will* is one of the three great divisions into which psychologists usually divide the powers of the mind (the others being cognition and feeling). I desire, I crave something; my intellect renders its decision; and my will carries it out.[10]

Conclusion

The fact that men are creatures of choice and the further fact that their choices are made in terms of some awareness of moral and ethical principles are firm evidences that they originated from a source that also had the capacity of making moral and ethical judgments. The atheist has a severe burden of proof at this point. In order for his position to be accepted, he must demonstrate how a morally responsible being could come from a purely materialistic source. Particularly impressive is the fact that man functions not merely in the direction of his strongest instincts, but that he often acts in a different direction. As C. S. Lewis put it, there is something within man that judges between his instincts and that decides which should be encouraged. Often it is the weaker instinct on which man acts, because it is ethically and morally superior to the other stronger instinct. This unique quality in man demands a moral architect and designer.

10. "Man Himself As Evidence," *The Evidence of God in an Expanding Universe,* ed. John Clover Monsma, pp. 197-199.

6

Aquinas and the Cosmological Arguments

Credit has generally been given to Thomas Aquinas, who lived in the late Middle Ages, as the one who gave the world the classical statement of the cosmological argument for the existence of God. Actually, this is a set of arguments based on one central idea: the existing cosmos is an undeniable evidence of a creator. The argument is based upon the general, universal observation that "Nothing comes from nothing." Everything must have some antecedent cause. Hence, reasoning from the world which obviously exists back to its creative cause, we find evidence that there must be some kind of creator. Aquinas stated his arguments in the following terms:

1. *Unmoved mover—prime mover.* Unless there is an "infinite regress," there must be a first mover. We human beings experience movement, but we know that there is no perpetual motion. There must be some force which started all movement. Therefore, there must be an unmoved mover or prime mover who started the universe. Thus, it is reasoned, God is the source behind the universe.

2. *Uncaused first cause.* Everything is an effect of some cause. There is no effect which did not have some antecedent cause behind it. Therefore, since there cannot be an "infinite regress," there must be an uncaused first cause.

3. *Necessary being.* Everything in existence today is also capable of not existing. All natural things are *contingent,* that

is, they are capable of being or not being. In a period of eternal time every contingent thing would cease to exist. Then, there would be no world, but since there is a world there must be some force behind it—God.

There is a story which dates back to the time when the statesman Benjamin Franklin was Ambassador of the United States to France. While living in Paris Franklin was a member of an elite literary social and scientific club. At certain of the meetings of this intellectual group, atheistic sentiments were expressed, leaving the impression that only the superstitious and uninformed still believed in God as the creator of the universe. At the next meeting of the group Benjamin Franklin brought a beautifully designed and executed model of the sun and our entire solar system. The earth and the other planets were in their proper relationship to the sun and to each other and of appropriate sizes. It was a masterpiece. Upon seeing it, one of the sophisticated members of the club asked, "Who made it?" Dryly, without the trace of a smile, Franklin responded, "No one. It just happened."

The cosmological argument has been impressive to many of the greatest minds of history. Chad Walsh, for example, writes the following:

> All that can be asked of anyone, theist or atheist, is that he show the balance of probability to be on his side. I believe in God. I believe in Him because I do not think that mere chance could account for the emergence of the first electrons or protons, or for the first atoms, or for the first amino acids, or the first protoplasm, or the first seed, or for the first brain. I believe in God because to me His divine existence is the only logical explanation of things as they are.[1]

Dr. Marlin Books Kreider, a physiologist, put the argument in these terms:

> Obviously no one in our present intellectual state will ever have proof of the method involved in creation. But

---

1. Chad Walsh, source unknown.

our scientific knowledge reveals so many improbabilities in the completely materialistic explanation that it is more rational to accept as the prime cause a form of special creation and the influence of an outside force. Albert Einstein, in recognizing this intelligent creative force, refers to it as "the illimitable superior reasoning power which is revealed in the incomprehensible universe. . . . I see at the beginning of the cosmic road—not eternal energy or matter, not "inscrutable fate," not a "fortuitous conflux of primordial elements," not "the great Unknown"—but the Lord God Almighty.[2]

Dr. Frank Allen, a biophysicist, analyzes the situation quite clearly in stating that there are only four alternatives:

Four solutions of its [the world's] origin may be proposed: first, that it is an illusion . . . second, that it spontaneously arose out of nothing; third, that it had no origin but has existed eternally; fourth, that it was created . . . either inanimate matter with its incorporated energy, or a Personal Creator, is eternal. No greater intellectual difficulty exists in the one concept than in the other. But the laws of thermo-dynamics (heat) indicate that the universe is running down. . . . In infinite time this state of entropy would already have happened. The hot sun and stars, the earth with its wealth of life, are complete evidence that the origin of the universe has occurred in *time,* at a fixed point of time, and therefore the universe must have been *created.*[3]

The second law of thermodynamics or entropy is emphasized by Dr. Edward Luther Kessel:

Science clearly shows that the universe could not have existed from all eternity. The law of entropy states that there is a continuous flow of heat from warmer to colder bodies. . . . Therefore the universe is headed for a time when the temperature will be universally uniform and there will be no more useful energy. Consequently there will be no more chemical and physical processes, and life

2. "Identifying Einstein's 'Creative Force,' " *The Evidence of God in an Expanding Universe,* ed. John Clover Monsma, p. 68.

3. "The Origin of the World—By Chance or Design?" Monsma, pp. 19-20.

itself will cease to exist. But because life is still going on, and chemical and physical processes are still in progress, it is evident that our universe could not have existed from eternity, else it would have long since run out of useful energy and ground to a halt. Therefore, quite unintentionally, science proves that our universe had a beginning. And in so doing it proves the reality of God, for whatever had a beginning did not begin of itself but demands a Prime Mover, a Creator, a God.[4]

Dr. John Cleveland Cothran, a mathematician and chemist, highlights a slightly different point:

Chemistry discloses that matter is ceasing to exist, some varieties exceedingly slowly, others exceedingly swiftly. Therefore the existence of matter is not eternal. Consequently matter must have had a beginning. Evidence from chemistry and other sciences indicates that this beginning was not slow and gradual; on the contrary, it was sudden, and the evidence even indicates the approximate time when it occurred. Thus at some rather definite time the material realm was *created* and ever since has been obeying *law,* not the dictates of chance.[5]

A word in defense of the believer's faith in the Biblical account of the origin of the earth was spoken by Dr. Wayne U. Ault, a geochemist:

. . . one's belief in God is largely a matter of faith, although this faith derives scientific support from indirect evidences of a "First Cause," and quite probably of a "Continuous Motivating Cause."

Faith is not something foreign to one in any field of human knowledge, but must be exercised especially by the physical scientists. . . . Subsequently, most of our knowledge is acquired by written history of past experience. . . . The Bible . . . has not, to my knowledge, been proved wrong in any detail of history or geography, although there are areas where our understanding is not complete. . . .

---

4. "Let's Look at Facts, Without Bent or Bias," Monsma, pp. 50-51.
5. "The Inescapable Conclusion," Monsma, pp. 41-42.

Just as faith is a necessary and normal part of one's existence, so the concept of God is essential to the completeness of man's being and philosophy. . . . But even from a non-Christian or non-religious viewpoint the concept of God is far more satisfactory than chance, and the marvelous order of the universe definitely indicates a God of order rather than random, uncontrolled chance.[6]

Conclusion

Dr. Merritt Stanley Congdon, a natural scientist, puts the matter very simply but very well: "Many years ago I saw a beautiful, cultivated rosebush in bloom beside a lonely road in Pennsylvania. . . . I *knew* intuitively that some mature human being had carefully planted it near his home."[7] As each of the men quoted in this chapter, and countless others who might have been quoted, point out, the obvious existence of our universe is a powerful evidence that there must have been a creative force that brought it into existence. The atheist's position that the universe just happened, with no creator behind it, is a position difficult to uphold in the face of all the evidence around us. Without exception, we find that "Nothing comes from nothing." Are we to believe that the universe in its entirety is an exception to this universal law? Whatever force it is that brought our universe into being, we call God.

---

6. "Concord Between Science and Faith," Monsma, pp. 208-210.
7. "The Lesson of the Rosebud," Monsma, p. 31.

7

The Teleological Argument

Just as Thomas Aquinas is credited with the classical statement of the cosmological argument, he is similarly credited with the definitive statement of the teleological argument for the existence of God. He classified this argument under a two-fold heading:

1. *Argument from design.* The universe demonstrates order and design, hence there must be a designer. The existence of order and system demands an orderer. Beauty, form, design, and purpose in nature all imply a creative mind, an intelligent architect. This idea of purpose in nature and in life processes is opposed to the view of mechanism. It suggests that the force that brought the universe into being is an intelligent, planning, thinking being.

2. *Argument from degrees of being.* The gradations of being, which are all about us, require that which has the quality in the superlative degree. The existence of something, or some quality, implies the absolute. Therefore, an orderly universe implies a perfect source from which the universe has come.

General Statements

The following statement appears in *The Mysterious Universe,* authored by Sir James Jeans, the world-renowned mathematician:

> . . . the universe begins to look more like a great thought than like a great machine. Mind no longer appears as an

accidental intruder into the realm of matter; we are beginning to suspect that we ought rather to hail it as the creator and governor of the realm of matter. . . . We discover that the universe shews evidence of a designing or controlling power that has something in common with our own individual minds. . . .[1]

Earlier he had written:

If the universe is a universe of thought, then its creation must have been an act of thought. Indeed the finiteness of time and space almost compel us, of themselves, to picture the creation as an act of thought. . . .[2]

Dr. John Cleveland Cothran, a mathematician and chemist, first quotes Lord Kelvin of England, one of the world's greatest physicists, who said, "If you think strongly enough, you will be forced by science to believe in God," and then presents these thoughts:

. . . study consistently has shown in the past, and still continues to show, that the behavior of even insensible matter is not at all haphazard, but on the contrary "obeys" definite "natural laws". . . . The discovery of atomic structure has now revealed that in all these examples of chemical behavior definite laws prevail, not haphazardness or chance. . . .

Yet, with all this seeming complexity, each atom of every one of the 102 elements consists of exactly the same three kinds of electrical particles: protons (positive), electrons (negative), and neutrons (each apparently some sort of combination of one proton with one electron). . . . So that all the millions of different kinds of substances, both elements and compounds, "simplify down" to three kinds of electrical particles which, in turn, appear to be only different forms of the one primary entity, electricity, which, finally, may be only a form or attribute or manifestation of the ultimate in simplicity: energy. . . . The material universe is unquestionably one of system and order, not chaos; of laws, not chance and haphazards.

1. New rev. ed. (New York: The Macmillan Company, 1942), pp. 186-187.
2. Jeans, p. 181.

Can any informed and reasoning intellect possibly believe that insensible and mindless matter just chanced to originate itself and all this system, then chanced to impose the system upon itself, whereafter this system just chances to remain imposed?[3]

Dr. Walter Oscar Lundberg, a physiologist and biochemist, provides us with his point of view:

The professional scientist has one special advantage over others, if he will but use it, in understanding the reality of God. The fundamental principles on which the methodology of his profession is based, are, in essence, an expression of God's existence. . . .

In short, the scientific method is founded on *orderliness* and *predictability* in natural phenomena. . . . Order and predictability in the framework of non-existence of God, that is, absence of rationality, is a meaningless contradiction. . . . When man abandons the concept of a God created in his image, and accepts Nature's revelations as evidence of man's creation in God's image, he has reached a threshold where he may begin to perceive God's majesty.[4]

Claude M. Hathaway, a consulting engineer, speaks out of his own experience:

. . . *design requires a designer*. . . . After years of work in the development and design of complicated mechanisms in electronic circuitry I have acquired a tremendous appreciation for *design* wherever I find it. . . . If my computer required a designer, how much more so did that complex physio-chemical-biological machine which is my human body—which in turn is but an extremely minute part of the well-nigh infinite cosmos? . . .

Sir Isaac Newton recognized that the universe was moving from order to dis-order; that it was approaching a uniform temperature; and from this he saw the necessity of an initial ordering or design . . . transfer in the opposite direction never occurs in Nature. This is the Second

3. "The Inescapable Conclusion," *The Evidence of God in an Expanding Universe*, ed. John Clover Monsma, pp. 37-41.

4. "Applying the Scientific Method," Monsma, pp. 55, 57.

law of Thermodynamics. . . . In simple terms, Boltz-
mann's Extended Second Law of Thermodynamics means
that Nature cannot design herself, because every physical
transformation must be accompanied by a loss in design.
In localized instances, order may progress from the simple to the complex, but only at the expense of a greater
loss of order elsewhere.

The universe is a tremendous "mass" (physics) of
order. Therefore a Great First Cause is required who is
not subject to the Second Law; who is, therefore, supernatural.[5]

Elmer W. Maurer, a research chemist, points out that the
scientific method depends upon the orderliness of the universe:

It is impossible for me to conceive the law and order of
the universe as being the result of pure chance. The odds
are simply too great. Law, order and intelligence go hand
in hand. Also, as a scientist I believe that God has
permanent control of His world. He sees to it that there is
fixedness and permanence in Nature's laws. When I step
into my laboratory I know that the laws that hold true
today will hold true tomorrow, and the next day, and as
long as the universe exists. Otherwise my life in the
laboratory would be a succession of quandaries; a life of
uncertainty and doubts, rendering all scientific activity
futile; in fact, impossible.[6]

Maurer further demonstrates the orderliness of the universe by referring to the periodic chart of the various known
elements:

In the periodic chart all the elements are grouped according to their atomic numbers. The atomic number is the
number of protons in the nucleus of the atom. Thus,
hydrogen, the simplest element, has one proton in its
nucleus; helium, two; lithium, three; and so on. . . . This
beautiful arrangement is hardly a matter of chance. . . .
What would be the odds of my getting 100 or so different
elements, each of which had its own characteristic prop-

erties and would fit into an orderly arrangement such as we have in the periodic chart?[7]

Finally, Maurer gives a statement of his own faith:

I have found nothing in natural science, in chemistry, that conflicts with the Bible. Nor do I find anything in the Bible that conflicts with science. The God of Genesis, I am convinced, is the sole answer to both the "genesis" and the unfailing, detailed management of the world.[8]

Dr. Russell Lowell Mixter, a zoologist, points out the orderly arrangement of the thousands of species of animals and plants:

There are probably a million species of animals on this earth. . . . Of plants one could find at least two hundred thousand species.

Order in such an array? There is order everywhere! Take just one of the one million species of animals. Each such species falls into groups, and each group can again be subdivided. But divide and subdivide as you will, the characteristics and similarities of the species will be found in all. One woodpecker, for example, has similarities that are common to all woodpeckers. . . .

If one basic material—flesh, protoplasm—can be found with infinitely varied arrangements of it in living things, and if at the same time a host of similarities can be found in a thousand-and-one different groupings, then it is certainly evident that back of it all is the thoughtful planning of a God who made the basic material and gave it the potentiality and directiveness of producing endless variations of itself. . . .

The same logical mind which notices that a human mind makes complicated things concludes that complicated living beings have been made by the Master Mind. No matter how much these beings vary among the members of one species, and no matter how much change there seems to have been in a species as it is traced back towards its ancestors, living and fossilized, one cannot fail to observe that it began with a well adapted creature.

7. Monsma, pp. 202-203.
8. Monsma, p. 206.

And a "creature" it was—the handiwork of a Creator! . . .
And what to me is an ever-shining, never-dimming truth
. . . is the fact that the God of the Bible and the God of
Nature are one and the same.[9]

Conclusion

Dr. Arthur H. Compton, Nobel Prize Winner in Physics,
states the case for faith simply but forcefully:

> For myself, faith begins with the realization that a su-
> preme intelligence brought the universe into being and
> created man. It is not difficult for me to have this faith,
> for it is incontrovertible that where there is a plan there is
> intelligence—an orderly, unfolding universe testifies to
> the truth of the most majestic statement ever uttered—
> "In the beginning God!"[10]

The teleological argument is very simple. The intricate
design found throughout the universe could not possibly have
come without some kind of supreme architect and designer
behind it. Where there is order there must be an orderer.
Where there is plan, there must be a planner.

---

9. "A Young Mystic Proceeds to Clear Thinking," Monsma, pp. 98-99.

10. From *Chicago Daily News* (April 12, 1936), as quoted by Roger J.
Voskuyl, "A Christian Interpretation of Science," in *Modern Science and Chris-
tian Faith,* by Members of the American Scientific Affiliation (Chicago: Scripture
Press, 1950), p. 3.

8

Design Demands a Designer

In addition to the general statements concerning the marvelous design which is built into the universe, I want to share with you some of the specific examples that have been impressive to me. In each of these cases, I consider it utterly impossible for a plan of such intricacy and sophistication to have developed by mere chance. It is difficult to see how an open mind can fail to recognize the hand of a creator in such masterpieces of design as these which follow. The one who does not believe in God has an insurmountable burden of explanation, it would seem, as to how each of these things might have come, if there is no God who designed them.

Dr. Thomas David Parks wrote of Whittaker Chambers, a former Communist who became a valuable employee of the State Department of the United States, as he described his very personal response to the orderliness of nature, as seen in his own small daughter. Parks says that Chambers, in his book, *Witness,* "tells of a simple incident which was probably the turning point of his life (and perhaps of the affairs of mankind). He was watching his little daughter and unconsciously became aware of the shape of her ears. He thought to himself how impossible that such delicate convolutions could have come about by chance. They could have been created only by pre-meditated design . . . [and] design presupposes God. . . ." Parks concluded, "I see order and design all about me in the inorganic world. . . . For me this design demands an intelligence, and this intelligence I call God."[1]

1. "Plain Water Will Tell You the Story," *The Evidence of God in an Expanding Universe,* ed. John Clover Monsma, pp. 73, 74.

Consider what Dr. A. Cressy Morrison, a physician and former president of the New York State Academy of Science, has to say:

> The evidence is strongly suggestive of this directive purpose back of everything. . . . We have found that the world is in the right place, that the crust is adjusted to within ten feet, and that if the ocean were a few feet deeper we would have no oxygen or vegetation. We have found that the earth rotates in twenty-four hours and that were this revolution delayed, life would be impossible. If the speed of the earth around the sun were increased or decreased materially, this history of life, if any, would be entirely different. We find that the sun is the one among thousands which could make our sort of life possible on earth, its size, density, temperature and the character of its rays all must be right, and are right. We find that the gases of the atmosphere are adjusted to each other and that a very slight change would be fatal. . . .
>
> Considering the bulk of the earth, its place in space and the nicety of the adjustments, the chances of some of these adjustments occurring is in the order of one to a million, and the chances of all of them occurring cannot be calculated even in the billions. The existence of these facts cannot, therefore, be reconciled with any of the laws of chance. It is impossible, then, to escape the conclusion that the adjustments of nature to man are far more amazing than the adjustments of man to nature. A review of the wonders of nature demonstrates beyond question that there are design and purpose in it all. A program is being carried out in all its infinite detail by the Supreme Being we call God.[2]

Dr. John William Klotz, a geneticist, tells the story of the yucca moth and yucca plant:

> This world of ours is so complex and so intricate that it could hardly have risen by chance. . . . One of the best known of these [intricacies] is the relationship between the yucca moth and the yucca plant, or Spanish bayonet.

2. From *Man Does Not Stand Alone* by A. Cressy Morrison. (New York: Fleming H. Revell Co., 1944), pp. 94, 95. Used with permission.

The yucca flower hangs down, and the pistil, or female part of the flower, is lower than the stamen, or male part. The stigma, however, the part of the flower specialized for the reception of pollen, is cup-shaped, and so arranged that it is impossible for the pollen to fall into it. Instead, the pollen must be transported by the female of the yucca moth who begins her work soon after sunset. She collects a quantity of pollen from the anthers of the plants and holds it in her specially constructed mouth parts. Then she flies to another yucca flower, pierces the ovary with her ovipositor, and after laying one or more eggs creeps down the style and stuffs the ball of pollen into the stigma. The plant produces a large number of seeds. Some are eaten by the larvae of the moth and some mature to perpetuate the plant.[3]

He then tells a similar story concerning the necessary relationship between the fig and a small wasp:

A similar situation exists in the relationship between the commercial fig and a group of small wasps. . . . When figs were first introduced into the United States, they did not produce the fruit. It was only after the wasp was brought in that it was possible to develop a commercially profitable fig industry.[4]

The story of the prison flower is also told by Dr. Klotz:

Very unusual are the prison flowers, such as the common jack-in-the-pulpit. This plant has two kinds of flower clusters, male and female. These are produced inside the pulpit which has a constriction about half way down. Usually pollination is effected by a tiny fly which comes in, gets past the constriction, and then finds himself trapped. Not only is the constriction in his way, but the sides of the pulpit are also waxy, preventing his getting a foothold. And so he buzzes around frantically, dusting himself with pollen in the process. Shortly thereafter the sides of the pulpit roughen, and he is able to crawl out, covered with pollen. If he visits next another male cluster, the process is repeated. But if he comes into a female

3. "Nature's Complexity and God," Monsma, pp. 77-78.
4. Monsma, pp. 78-79.

flower, it is possible that he will not escape. For his frantic buzzing dusts the flower with pollen, and this time the plant is not interested in his escaping. It is to the plant's advantage to have him escape from the male pulpit to carry the pollen with him. The plant seems unconcerned, however, about his escape from a female flower.[5]

At this point he gives us his conclusion:

All of these instances testify to the existence of God. It is hard to believe that these could have arisen by blind chance: their existence is due to God's directing hand and to His creative power.[6]

Dr. Klotz also speaks of the remarkable balance of nature that is observed throughout the world:

. . . . man to his regret has attempted to make changes in the balance of Nature. . . . [In Australia] in an attempt to improve Nature, Thomas Austin imported some 24 European rabbits, back in 1859. The results were unfortunate, for there were no natural enemies in Australia to keep the rabbits in check. They multiplied beyond all expectation and did serious damage, destroying the grass on which the sheep fed. . . .

A moment ago instances were mentioned testifying to the *existence* of God. What has been described just now is a powerful testimony to God's *wisdom*. The balances which He has established are delicate, and man . . . should be very hesitant to try to *improve* Nature's balances—he will find that his human intelligence is no match for that of Nature's God.[7]

Dr. Cecil Boyce Hamann, a biologist, mentions the case of the remarkable Baltimore Oriole:

. . . how about the nest of the Baltimore Oriole? Who taught him that fine workmanship? Why is there such a similarity of pattern? To answer "instinct" is an easy way

---

5. Monsma, p. 79.
6. Monsma, p. 79.
7. Monsma, pp. 80-81.

out, but is it an adequate answer? What are instincts? Some say unlearned behavior. Is it not more logical to see God working in these creations of His according to principles concerning which we have as yet only the slightest of clues?[8]

Dr. Hamann turns to an entirely different area to find an equally amazing evidence of design:

> . . . an amoeba slowly oozes along, almost imperceptibly a smaller organism is enveloped, and even as we watch, it is digested, assimilated, and waste left behind. As we continue to watch we see the amoeba actually pull itself into two parts, with each half re-forming itself into a complete animal. Here we have seen one cell carrying on all of the vital activities of life for which larger animals require thousands or millions of cells. Evidently more than chance has been responsible for this wonderfully made animal, infinitesimally small as it is.[9]

A remarkable characteristic of water is cited by Dr. Thomas David Parks, a research chemist:

> Water is the only known substance which becomes lighter as it freezes. This is tremendously important to life. Because of it, ice floats instead of sinking to the bottom of lakes and rivers and gradually forming a solid mass. On the top of the water it forms a layer of insulation to maintain the water below at a temperature above freezing. Fish and other marine life are preserved and the ice melts rapidly in the spring. . . . Personally, I have found my explanation of these marvels—a satisfying explanation—in relating Nature's order to a Supreme Intelligence and its design to a Supreme Designer, and in it all I see more than cold, rational planning—I see the concern and love of a Creator for His creatures.[10]

The remarkable qualities of the cell are pointed out by Dr. Russell Charles Artist, a biologist and botanist:

---

8. "Of Flowers and the Baltimore Oriole," Monsma, p. 220.
9. Monsma, p. 221.
10. "Plain Water Will Tell You the Story," Monsma, pp. 75-76.

Each of the cells shows a magnificent structure. . . .
Each cell seems to be a unit in itself, each apparently
capable of carrying on its life activities independently of
others like itself. . . . Each cell performs these activities
with a precision that by comparison makes the running of
even the finest watch a clumsy affair. . . . When we ask
concerning the living cell: "How did this microscopic but
amazing functional unit come to have its present form?"
or "How was it set in motion?" we are confronted with
formidable, even insuperable, difficulties in trying to account for its beginning and, for that matter, its continued
functioning, unless we maintain with reason and logic
that an intelligence, a mind, brought it into existence.
This Mind, this Supreme Intelligence, as contrasted with
unthinking Matter, is God. . . . Just so the Organizer of
the universe is necessary to the creation of a cell—and to
the minds of reasoning men searching for a first
cause. . . .

I maintain that each of these single cells (each a system
so intricate and delicate that its complete functioning has
so far escaped our study), and all the trillions of them on
this earth, definitely present a justifiable inference—one
of Mind, or Intelligence, or Thought which we call God.
Science both admits and accepts this inference.[11]

Even more impressive is Dr. Artist's account of certain
phenomena connected with human birth:

In the very act of being born every human being gives a
remarkable demonstration of the fact that we are "fear-
fully and wonderfully made" (Ps. 139:14, AV) and at the
same time points up a problem in biology for which there
can be no adequate explanation other than that there are
of necessity intelligent planning and design.

The average person on the street knows, of course, that
his heart is like a double pump, the right side containing
impure blood and the left side containing only pure or
oxygenated blood, which has come from the lungs. Two
separate systems of circulation keep the two types of
blood from mixing. The right side is called the systemic
system and the left side the pulmonary system. The adult

---

11. "Trillions of Cells Speak Their Message," Monsma, pp. 119-124.

heart is thus arranged to keep these two completely separated in order for the body to function properly.

But the unborn child has no need for this complete
separation of the two types of blood. The mother does
the breathing for the embryo (the lungs are not even
inflated in the unborn child), and the mother's blood-
stream provides for the aeration of the child's blood.
Thus, there are two short circuits in the system of circulation of the embryo before birth. One of these is a small
opening between the right auricle and the left auricle of
the fetal heart—an opening right through the wall, known
as the *foramen ovale,* which allows the blood to flow
uninterrupted through the two cavities. The other bypass
in the system is a short and thick vessel, equipped with a
tough sheet of smooth muscle, which connects the pulmonary artery with the great aortic arch that carries
oxygenated blood to all parts of the body. These two
short circuits, prepared to serve the unborn fetus, are
destined to be changed at the time of birth and are never
used again.

The sequence and precision of it all are wonders in
themselves and, with God ruled out, problems of con-
siderable dimensions. With God recognized, they become
parts of His creational design.

The opening between the two auricles, the *foramen
ovale,* is in embryonic life guarded by flaps of tissue that
permit the flow of blood through the opening. At birth,
and instantaneously, because of certain pressure relationships, the flaps are closed, never to open again. The exact
nature of these pressure relationships is not known. We
are facing an unsolved problem. Eventually new tissue
grows across the opening, and in the majority of people
this shortcut is completely sealed off in adult life. Otherwise, there would be a condition called leakage of the
heart, which would mean a mixing of pure and impure
blood. In about one-fifth of the population, however, a
tiny opening remains to mark the spot of this shortcut
that once existed before birth. It is indeed a marvel of
unique design that can provide for a system that operates
efficiently through embryonic life and then, at the moment of birth, causes a closing of this opening so that it
remains sealed throughout adult life.

Now we come to the muscle that *contracts only once*
during the entire duration of life. It is the same smooth

muscle which occurs on the short bypass from the pulmonary artery to the aorta. As soon as the lungs fill with air at the moment of birth, the contracting muscle causes the vessel to close off completely. This causes the blood to flood into the lungs to be aerated with oxygen. The action of the muscle is effected by some unknown stimulus—one of our unsolved problems. The muscle eventually degenerates and disappears.

After birth the breathing and circulation are similiar to those of the adult body. One could not find a better example of wise planning and intelligent design than in these two adjustments, which are made by every fetus at birth.

That it is absolutely essential for the two to function properly—without training or research—lies in the sobering fact that after failure there are no second chances. As the lungs have not inflated before in the unborn child, there must be no slipup in this at the time when the baby must breathe for itself. Also, that these two shortcuts should be closed correctly the *first and only time* means the difference between life and death.

Parents who await the birth of their child can derive strength and joy from the knowledge that in the vast majority of cases God's creational design works out wonderfully and that for Him problems do not exist.[12]

Conclusion

With examples like these before us, how is it possible to think that our universe came by a mere chance combination of atoms? Of all of the arguments for the existence of God, none overwhelms the mind so completely as the teleological argument from design. One may not choose to worship God, or even to acknowledge the overwhelming evidence of His remarkable creation, but I do not see how he can do it and claim to be a respecter of evidence.

In some of the instances sighted, the characteristics described could not have been achieved through a long, slow,

12. "The Wonder of Life and Its Endless Varieties," *Behind the Dim Unknown,* ed. John Clover Monsma (New York: G. P. Putnam's Sons, 1966), pp. 21-23.

gradual development, covering aeons of time. The foramen ovale in the baby's heart must be closed instantly and forever, or the child cannot live. It must work perfectly the very first time. The muscle that first causes the baby to breathe could hardly have developed gradually over long periods of time, since it had to operate perfectly on the first occasion or there would have been no other occasions. Similarly, how could plants and insects which depend upon each other for survival have developed along separate lines through vast ages of evolutionary growth before discovering each other?

In a sense, those who do not believe in the creative hand of God are asking us to believe that through a long evolutionary process these remarkable phenomena developed through the various stages until ultimately the perfected stage which we now observe arrived. This is about as logical as asking us to believe that a man can jump across a wide ditch, a foot at a time. He either goes all the way, or he does not go at all. Until someone is able to explain all of these remarkable phenomena without a creator God behind them, we must continue to believe that there is a God who planned all of them.

9

Consequences of Skepticism

The most elementary logic tells us that a thoughtful person will carefully examine the destination at the end of the road before he begins to travel the road. If a road does not lead to the destination to which a person wishes to go, he ought certainly to choose a different road. It is with this in mind that we pause to suggest the consequences of skepticism. Through the centuries there have been a number of prominent men in the field of philosophy, government, and literature, who have set down quite carefully their own feelings concerning their lack of faith in God. In most instances it is indeed a dismal picture—one that could hardly be described as inviting. Listen to a few of these men as they describe their own disillusionment. Voltaire, the noted French revolutionary thinker:

> Strike out a few sages, and the crowd of human beings is nothing but a horrible assemblage of unfortunate criminals, and the globe contains nothing but corpses. I tremble to have to complain once more of the Being of Beings in casting an attentive eye over this terrible picture. I wish I had never been born.[1]

Goethe, the German philosopher, expressing his despondency:

> I have ever been esteemed one of Fortune's chiefest favourites; nor will I complain or find fault with the

---

1. "Dialogues," II, 194, in John Cairns, *Unbelief in the Eighteenth Century* (Edinburgh: Adam and Charles Black, 1881), p. 141.

course my life has taken. Yet, truly, there has been nothing but toil and care; and I may say that, in all my seventy-five years, I have never had a month of genuine comfort. It has been the perpetual rolling of a stone, which I have always had to raise anew. . . . Men will become more clever and more acute, but not better, happier, and stronger in action, or at least only at epochs.[2]

Renan, the French writer, expressing his view quite briefly: "We are living on the perfume of an empty vase."[3]

Another Frenchman, Theodore Jouffroy, describing in an intimate, personal way his own disillusionment:

. . . I knew then that at the bottom of myself there was nothing left standing, that all I had believed about myself, about God, and about my destiny in this life and in that to come, I now believed no more. This moment was frightful; and when, towards morning, I threw myself exhausted upon my bed, it seemed to me as if I could feel my former life, so cheerful and complete, die away, and before me there opened another life, dark and dispeopled, where henceforth I was to live alone, alone with my fatal thought which had just exiled me thither, and which I was tempted to curse.[4]

Fredreich Nietzsche, the German philosopher who so influenced Adolf Hitler, expressing his disappointments:

Where is—*my* home? For it do I ask and seek, and have sought, but have not found it. O eternal everywhere, O eternal nowhere, O eternal—in-vain![5]

H. G. Wells, the noted author: "There is no way out, or around, or through. It is the end."[6]

---

2. Eckerman and Soret, *Conversations of Goethe,* trans. John Oxenford, rev. ed. (London: G. Bell and Sons, 1906), pp. 58, 345.

3. James Orr, *The Christian View of God and the World,* 3rd ed. (New York: Charles Scribner's Sons, 1897), p. 67.

4. *Les Nouveaux Melanges Philosophies,* pp. 112-115.

5. *Thus Spake Zarathustra,* trans. John Common, The Modern Library (New York: Boni and Liveright, Inc., 1917), p. 274.

6. *London Sunday Express* (March, 1946), quoted by James D. Bales, *Atheism's Faith and Fruits* (Boston: W. A. Wilde Co., 1951), p. 75.

Robert Ingersoll, the famous nineteenth-century American orator, delivering the eulogy at his brother's grave:

Life is a narrow vale between the cold and barren peaks of two eternities. We strive in vain to look beyond the heights. We cry aloud, and the only answer is the echo of a wailing cry. From the voiceless lips of the unreplying dead there comes no word; but in the night of death hope sees a star and listening love can hear the rustle of a wing. He who sleeps here, when dying, mistaking the approach of death for the return of health, whispered with his latest breath, "I am better now." Let us believe, in spite of doubts and dogmas and tears and fears, that these dear words are true of all the countless dead.[7]

Mark Twain, revealing his own inner despair:

A myriad of men are born; they labor and sweat and struggle for bread; they squabble and scold and fight; they scramble for little mean advantages over each other. Age creeps upon them; infirmities follow; shames and humiliations bring down their prides and their vanities. Those they love are taken from them and the joy of life is turned to aching grief. The burden of pain, care, misery, grows heavier year by year. At length ambition is dead; pride is dead; vanity is dead; longing for release is in their place. It comes at last—the only unpoisoned gift earth ever had for them—and they vanish from a world where they were of no consequence; where they achieved nothing; where they were a mistake and a failure and a foolishness; where they have left no sign that they have existed—a world which will lament them a day and forget them forever. Then another myriad takes their place and copies all they did and goes along the same profitless road and vanishes as they vanished—to make room for another and another and a million other myriads to follow the same arid path through the same desert and accomplish what the first myriad and all the myriads that came after it accomplished—nothing![8]

7. *Complete Lectures of R. G. Ingersoll,* compiler unknown (Chicago: J. Regan & Co., n.d.), p. 60.
8. *The Autobiography of Mark Twain,* ed. Charles Neider (New York: Harper & Brothers, Publishers, 1959), p. 191.

The late Bertrand Russell, the brilliant philosopher of our own age, expressing his views:

> The life of Man is a long march through the night, surrounded by invisible foes, tortured by weariness and pain, towards a goal that few can hope to reach, and where none may tarry long.[9]
>
> That Man is the product of causes which had no prevision of the end they were achieving; that his origin, his growth, his hopes and fears, his loves and his beliefs, are but the outcome of accidental collocations of atoms; that no fire, no heroism, no intensity of thought and feeling, can preserve an individual life beyond the grave; that all the labours of the ages, all the devotion, all the inspiration, all the noonday brightness of human genius, are destined to extinction in the vast death of the solar system, and that the whole temple of Man's achievement must inevitably be buried beneath the débris of a universe in ruins—all these things, if not quite beyond dispute, are yet so nearly certain, that no philosophy which rejects them can hope to stand.[10]

Differing from those just mentioned, Michael Faraday had many questions and doubts about the existence of God and the validity of the religion of the Bible during his lifetime, but as he approached death, his views changed. Of him John Clover Monsma tells this story:

> A case by itself [a doubter who changed his views at death] was that of Michael Faraday, world-renowned English chemist and physicist, who had been theorizing and speculating and building thought structures all his life. One day, in 1867, he lay on his deathbed, and a friend and colleague asked the great scientist, "Faraday, what are your speculations *now?*" "Speculations?" repeated the dying man. "Speculations? I have none! Thank God, I am not resting my dying head upon *speculations*. I *know* whom I have believed and am persuaded that He is able to keep that which I have committed unto Him against that day."[11]

---

9. "A Free Man's Worship," in *Mysticism and Logic and Other Essays,* 7th ed. (London: George Allen & Unwin Ltd., 1932), p. 56.

10. Russell, pp. 47-48.

11. "Editor's Introduction," *The Evidence of God in an Expanding Universe,* p. 14.

A chart (with slight modification) prepared by Virgil R. Trout[12] contrasts sharply the end results of believing in God with those of not believing in God. He demonstrates clearly that the results of faith, or doubt, are far-reaching indeed.

CHRISTIAN	SKEPTIC
I. *Philosophies of History*	
Beginning by God	Beginning???
Purpose of God	Force???
Judgment	Ending???
II. *Philosophies of Politics*	
God Involved in History	No God (Referee or Umpire)
Man in God's Image	Man (Merely a Graduate Beast)
Man ◢◣ State (triangle: Man at apex, State at base)	State ▽ Man (inverted triangle: State at top, Man at base)
III. *Philosophies of Ethics*	
God Has Revealed Himself to Man	Man Is the Highest Authority
Man Is Capable of Making Choices	No Absolute Right or Wrong
Therefore: Some Actions are Right Some Actions are Wrong	Truth Relative: Vogue of the Moment
Man Is Responsible for His Actions	Heredity Plus Environment Means Man Is Not Responsible
IV. *Philosophies of Science*	
God Created the Universe	Universe Originated by Chance
The Universe Is Orderly	Governed by Impersonal "Laws of Nature"
Man Is God's Steward, Served by Politics, Science, Art	Science Is the Discovery of These Laws, So Man Is Subject to Science
V. *Philosophies of Religion*	
Man Is a Worshiping Being	Man's Desire to Worship is a Sign of Immaturity
Worship Is Personal Communion With God, the Creator	The Result Is the Worship of Things and of Man Himself

12. *Christian Evidences* (Austin, Texas: R. B. Sweet Co., Inc., 1963), pp. 23-29.

Conclusion

In the March, 1970 issue of the *Reader's Digest,* there appeared an article by David Raphael Klein, entitled, "Is There a Substitute For God?" This article, to an unusually high degree, contains what I believe would be the ultimate consequences if a significant portion of our people were to give up orthodox faith in God and in the Christian religion. Klein began by calling attention to the trend in Western society which would remove God as a personal force, a decider of man's fate, and as the creator of the universe. Under this view sin becomes a relative, sociological matter, or even a pure fiction.

Klein writes of those who have exchanged their faith in God for these views:

> He still believed in right and wrong, and he still knew when he was doing wrong, as he saw it, but he no longer believed he had offended God by it or incurred His punishment. In fact, there *was* no punishment; he only felt guilty, or resolved not to do wrong again. The difference between living this way, and trying to live righteously because God commands it is profound. A man could now do anything he wanted, subject only to the laws of the land and his own judgment. Yet this judgment he had formed in part from parents and institutions whose outlook was still religious. So, although he has denied the basis of the morality of his forebears, such a man still acts in its terms. He obeys the Commandments without believing they were commanded; he speaks of right and wrong in the framework of conviction he no longer possesses; he acts according to a Judeo-Christian ethic, although he has abjured the belief.[13]

For a time the moral and ethical behavior would remain much as before, though for different reasons. Ultimately, however, as Klein further says,

---

13. Klein, pp. 51-52.

He finds his life-held standards dissolving beneath him. Cynicism plagues him, but he cannot refute it; he rejects pure hedonism as a way of life, but he has no philosophy with which to dispute its claims. And, beyond all this, another trouble bewilders, wounds, frightens and embitters him, in the face of which he is as impotent as toward all the rest: the rebellion of his children against him.[14]

The man who has abandoned religious faith has no answer to the question, "What is the meaning of man's existence?" If there is no real meaning or purpose in man's existence, how can a parent convince a child that the taking of drugs, or even committing suicide, is wrong? When faith in God is abandoned, the old, general, moral standards will continue to hold for a brief generation, but then will come the deluge. In America, we are beginning to reap the bitter fruits of a generation which has to an increasing degree lost faith in God. When the young are told that our entire civilization is founded on nothing morally solid they find themselves without a foundation upon which to stand, standards by which to live, and goals toward which to strive. They can really be sure of nothing. No wonder they are often angry, rebellious, violent, and destructive.

The consequences of skepticism are frightening. Surely no one would want to go down a road that leads ultimately to this kind of destination. I am in full agreement, however, that one cannot choose, in matters of faith, to go only in the direction in which he wishes to go, for essentially he must go in the direction toward which the evidence points. He must be loyal to truth. It has seemed legitimate, however, to give at least some indication of the ultimate destiny to which skepticism leads. This is defensible only when there is the conviction, which I confidently hold, that the evidence solidly supports the idea that there is a God.

---

14. Klein, p. 53.

10

Consequences of Faith

How dismal are the consequences of skepticism. In contrast, how bright are the consequences of faith. Let us examine the statements of some of those who have confidently believed in the God revealed in nature and in the Scriptures. As we found ourselves in the dark of night in the past chapter, we now find ourselves in the brilliance of the noonday sun.

First note the words of the psalmist, David, in his greatest Psalm, the twenty-third:

> The Lord is my shepherd; I shall not want.
> He maketh me to lie down in green pastures: he leadeth me beside the still waters.
> He restoreth my soul: he leadeth me in the paths of righteousness for his name's sake.
> Yea, though I walk through the valley of the shadow of death, I will fear no evil: for thou art with me; thy rod and thy staff they comfort me.
> Thou preparest a table before me in the presence of mine enemies: thou anointest my head with oil; my cup runneth over.
> Surely goodness and mercy shall follow me all the days of my life: and I will dwell in the house of the Lord for ever (KJV).

In the New Testament we find statements from the apostle Paul particularly significant, since he was a young man of unusual brilliance of mind, as well as one who possessed unusual skill in speaking and writing. To the young man Timothy he wrote:

> For which cause I suffer also these things: yet I am not ashamed; for I know him whom I have believed, and I am persuaded that he is able to guard that which I have committed unto him against that day (II Tim. 1:12).

In the final chapter of his letter to the church at Philippi Paul wrote:

> Rejoice in the Lord always: again I will say, Rejoice. . . . In nothing be anxious; but in everything by prayer and supplication with thanksgiving let your requests be made known unto God. And the peace of God, which passeth all understanding, shall guard your hearts and your thoughts in Christ Jesus. . . . Not that I speak in respect of want: for I have learned, in whatsoever state I am, therein to be content. . . . I can do all things in him that strengtheneth me (Phil. 4:4-8, 11, 13).

One of the greatest speeches of the entire Bible was Paul's message to the Athenians on Mars Hill:

> Ye men of Athens, in all things I perceive that ye are very religious. For as I passed along, and observed the objects of your worship, I found also an altar with this inscription, TO AN UNKNOWN GOD. What therefore ye worship in ignorance, this I set forth unto you. The God that made the world and all things therein, he, being Lord of heaven and earth, dwelleth not in temples made with hands; neither is he served by men's hands, as though he needed anything, seeing he himself giveth to all life, and breath, and all things; and he made of one every nation of men to dwell on all the face of the earth, having determined their appointed seasons, and the bounds of their habitation; that they should seek God, if haply they might feel after him and find him, though he is not far from each one of us: for in him we live, and move, and have our being; as certain even of your own poets have said,
> For we are also his offspring.
> Being then the offspring of God, we ought not to think that the Godhead is like unto gold, or silver, or stone, graven by art and device of man. The times of ignorance therefore God overlooked; but now he commandeth men that they should all everywhere repent: inasmuch as he

hath appointed a day in which he will judge the world in righteousness by the man whom he hath ordained; whereof he hath given assurance unto all men, in that he hath raised him from the dead (Acts 17:22-31).

One of the greatest preachers of this century was T. B. Larimore. After a long lifetime of preaching the message of Christ with matchless skill to thousands of people and with great effect, he wrote in his declining years these words of serene confidence and trust:

> My faith has never been stronger; my hope has never been brighter; my head has never been clearer; my heart has never been calmer; my life has never been purer. I love all; I hate none. My love for some lifts my soul into the realm of the sublime. I am willing to die today; I am willing to live a thousand years, to tell the old, old story of Jesus and his love. My friends are dearer to me; association with them is sweeter to me; my sympathy for suffering souls is stronger; my love for all the pure, the true, the beautiful, the good, and the sublime—from the bud, the blossom, the babe, up to Him from whom all blessings flow—is truer, tenderer, sweeter, than ever before. . . . I sleep soundly, dream sweetly, and "rejoice evermore." "The word" is sweeter and stronger to me than ever before. O it is delightful to love and be loved, and to do whatsoever duty demands! My vanity is all gone. What the people say does not bother me. I'll never waver, but always to the right be true.[1]

Conclusion

As we of the twentieth century examine all of the various theories concerning life and as we choose from among them that which seems most meaningful for our own lives, I am confident that faith in God and acceptance of the Christian religion offers the greatest promise of happiness and peace of mind. Of all the views known by man, the teachings of Christ offer the finest foundation upon which to build an individual

---

1. *Letters and Sermons,* ed. F. D. Srygley (Nashville, Tenn.: Gospel Advocate Company, 1900), pp. 140-142.

life, a happy home, a meaningful relationship with other people, a smoothly functioning nation, and a better world. We believe that the evidence in the universe about us makes it possible for us to hold this view of faith in God honestly and without reservation. We are aware that, as Harvey W. Everest has said, "We cannot believe unless belief is more rational than unbelief."[2] Therefore, for any belief, the rational ground for that belief must be presented. The scales must tip in the direction of faith, if we are to accept a point of controversy. We believe that the evidence does tip the scales solidly in favor of belief in God and the Christian religion.

Before leaving this chapter, consider the statement of Theodore Christlieb:

> The denial of the existence of God involves a perfectly monstruous hypothesis; it is, when looked at more closely, an unconscionable assumption. Before one can say that the world is without a God, he must first have become thoroughly conversant with the whole world. He must have searched through the universe of suns and stars, as well as the history of all ages; he must have wandered through the whole realm of space and time in order to be able to assert with truth, "Nowhere has a trace of God been found!" He must be acquainted with every force in the whole universe; for should but one escape him, that very one might be God. He must be able to count up with certainty all the causes of existence; for were there *one* that he did not know, that one might be God. He must be in absolute possession of all the elements of truth, which form the whole body of our knowledge; for else the one factor which he did not possess might be *just the very* truth that there is a God. If he does not know and cannot explain everything that has happened in the course of ages, just the very point which he does not know, and is unable to explain, may involve the instrumentality of a God. In short, *to be able to affirm authoritatively that no God exists, a man must be omniscient and omnipresent, that is, he himself must be God;* and then after all there would be one. You see in this the monstrosity of the atheistic hypothesis, that it is

---

2. *The Divine Demonstration* p. 13.

possible to prove the non-existence of God. Atheism depends as much, and more, than Theism on *faith,* that is, on assumptions which cannot be proved.[3]

Dr. Donald Henry Porter, mathematician and physicist, points out that absolute proof is possible neither in the physical realm nor the spiritual. Both require faith:

> If one could prove that there is a God in the same sense that one proves the Theorem of Pythagoras in geometry then belief in God would be compulsory. That kind of proof, I believe, does not exist. On the other hand, science is composed in the main of unproved laws or principles. This lack of proof does not prohibit one from using these laws as they might apply to various situations. It is not reasonable to expect proofs in the realm of the supernatural when proofs in the natural are lacking.[4]

Finally, I would point out, that in religion we accept one big miracle (God) and everything else makes sense. In atheism man must accept an endless series of little miracles in order to explain existence. Ultimately, man must choose between eternal mind or eternal matter. Eternal mind is the better, more rational, choice.

---

3. *Modern Doubt and Christian Belief,* trans. W. U. Weitbrecht, ed. T. L. Kingsbury (New York: Charles Scribner's Sons, 1878), pp. 143-144.
4. "The Answer to the Unanswered Questions," *The Evidence of God in an Expanding Universe,* ed. John Clover Monsma, p. 43.

Part Three

How the Universe Began

If the universe is a universe of thought, then its creation must have been an act of thought. ... Mind no longer appears as an accidental intruder into the realm of matter; we are beginning to suspect that we ought rather to hail it as the creator and governor of the realm of matter. ... We are not so much strangers or intruders in the universe as we at first thought.

—Sir James Jeans

11

The Limitations of Science

Scientists generally acknowledge that they do not know absolutely how the universe and life originated. The whole realm of science is the study of things as they are. Science can examine and analyze present processes and materials, but science is not in a position to say how things actually came into existence. Its observations necessarily were begun long after the beginning of the universe. Scientists can make intelligent guesses and offer hypotheses, but they are not in a position to speak with the same authority about how the universe began as they are to speak about the present operation of the universe. A number of prominent men of science have made this distinction quite clear.

Dr. Paul Amos Moody, a leading evolutionist of today, authored a book, *Introduction to Evolution,* that is probably used in more colleges and universities as a textbook than any other book. He answers the question, "How did life on earth begin?" in this way:

> The answer is that we do not know and probably never will. The origin of life occurred more than three *billion* years ago and was not the type of happening to leave a clear indication of its course of events in the fossil record. Why, then, do we discuss the question at all? The best we can do is to point out what *might* have happened.[1]

Dr. Asa Gray, for many years professor of botany at Harvard, had written essentially the same thing some years earlier. He spoke of

1. 3rd ed. (New York: Harper & Row, Publishers, 1970), p. 115.

a beginning which was wholly beyond the ken and scope of science, which is concerned with questions about how things go on, and has nothing to say as to how they absolutely began.[2]

Ernest Haeckel was in full agreement:

The process of creation as the coming into existence of matter is completely beyond human comprehension and can therefore never become a subject of scientific inquiry.[3]

Dr. L. L. Woodruff, while Professor of Biology at Yale, made the point that it is impossible to gain satisfying evidence about the origin of life:

Biologists are at the present time absolutely unable, and probably will be for all time unable to obtain empirical evidence of any of the crucial questions relating to the origin of life on the earth.[4]

Lorus J. and Margery Milne speak of the hypothetical nature of man's theories about how life began:

The transformation of an initially lifeless planet into one supporting life . . . is a change that must always remain hypothetical.[5]

Hans Gaffron comments:

Part of the fascination . . . stems from the apparent necessity to believe in events which happened only once—tantamount to acts of special creation. . . .[6]

2. *Natural Science and Religion* (New York: Charles Scribner's Sons, 1880), p. 38.

3. *The History of Creation,* Eng. trans. (London: 1925), I, 8, as quoted by Wilbur M. Smith, *Therefore Stand* (Boston: W. A. Wilde Co., 1945), p. 274.

4. *The Evolution of the Earth and Its Inhabitants,* p. 107, in Smith, *Therefore Stand,* p. 274.

5. *The Biotic World and Man,* 3rd ed. (Englewood Cliffs, N.J.: Prentice-Hall, 1965), p. 568.

6. "The Origin of Life," in *Evolution After Darwin,* ed. Sol Tax (Chicago: The University of Chicago Press, 1960), I, 51.

Sir Oliver Lodge cited the lack of any real knowledge in this area:

> It [science] has not yet witnessed the origin of the smallest trace of life from dead matter: all life, so far as has been watched, proceeds from antecedent life. . . . But ultimate origins are inscrutable. Let us admit, as scientific men, that of real origin, even of the simplest thing, we know nothing; not even of a pebble.[7]

Thomas H. Huxley, a leading evolutionist, admitted the limitations of science:

> It appears to me that the scientific investigator is wholly incompetent to say anything at all about the first origin of the material universe. The whole power of his organon vanishes when he has to step beyond the chain of natural causes and effects. No form of nebular hypothesis that I know of is necessarily connected with any view of the origination to the nebular substance.[8]

He further said,

> To say, in the admitted absence of evidence, that I have any belief as to the mode in which the existing forms of life have originated, would be using words in a wrong sense.[9]

That origins are outside the realm in which science operates is pointed out by Drs. Donald Robertson and John Sinclair:

> In conclusion, it is interesting to note that it is impossible to demonstrate God's creative activity from within the realm of scientific discovery, just as it is also impossible to demonstrate his sustaining activity. However, these relationships of God to his creation are not anti-scientific

---

7. *Science and Immortality* (New York: Moffat, Yard and Company, 1908), pp. 17, 26.
8. *Nineteenth Century*, Feb., 1886, p. 202, in Smith, *Therefore Stand*, p. 274.
9. "Presidential Address, British Assoc. for Advancement of Science," 1870, *Selected Works. Discourses Biological and Geological*, p. 259, in Smith, *Therefore Stand*, p. 564.

just because they cannot be demonstrated by science. They are concepts that are outside of the realm in which science operates and thus science has little if anything to say about their validity. These are questions that must be answered by faith.[10]

Louis Pasteur, the pioneer in medicine, made a significant comment along the same line:

. . . in the face of these great problems, these eternal subjects of man's solitary meditation, there are only two attitudes of mind: one created by faith, the belief in a solution given by Divine revelation; and that of tormenting the soul by the pursuit of impossible explanations.[11]

This interesting comment was made by Lord Kelvin:

. . . I cannot admit that, with regard to the origin of life, science neither affirms nor denies Creative Power. Science positively affirms Creative Power. It is not in dead matter that we live and move and have our being, but in the creating and directing Power which science compels us to accept as an article of belief. . . . There is nothing between absolute scientific belief in a Creative Power, and the acceptance of the theory of a fortuitous concourse of atoms. . . . Forty years ago I asked Liebig, walking somewhere in the country, if he believed that the grass and flowers that we saw around us grew by mere chemical forces. He answered, "No, no more than I could believe that a book of botany describing them could grow by mere chemical forces." . . . Do not be afraid of being free thinkers! If you think strongly enough you will be forced by science to the belief in God, which is the foundation of all religion. You will find science not antagonistic but helpful to religion.[12]

Dr. W. F. Albright, dean of American archeologists, spoke favorably of the Biblical account of creation:

---

10. "Genetics," *Evolution and Christian Thought Today,* ed. Russell L. Mixter (Grand Rapids, Michigan: Wm. B. Eerdmans Publishing Company, 1959), p. 91. Used with permission.
11. In L. Descours: *Pasteur and His Work,* Eng. trans. (London: 1922), p. 206, quoted by Smith, *Therefore Stand,* pp. 275-276.
12. *Nineteenth Century and After,* LIII, June, 1903, pp. 1068-1069.

The account of creation which we find is unique in ancient literature. It undoubtedly reflects an advanced monotheistic point of view, with a sequence of creative phases which is so rational that modern science cannot improve on it, given the same language and the same range of ideas in which to state its conclusions. In fact, modern scientific cosmogonies show such a disconcerting tendency to be short-lived that it may be seriously doubted whether science has yet caught up with the Biblical story.[13]

Conclusion

The point made in this brief chapter is simply that men of science are not in a position to say authoritatively how the universe came into being and how life on earth began. They can advance their hypotheses and express their guesses, but there is no way for the methodology of science, which is the examination of things as they now function, to determine absolutely how they began. It is important that we keep this in mind.

---

13. Herbert Christian Alleman and Elmer E. Flack, *Old Testament Commentary* (Philadelphia: Muhlenberg Press, 1948), p. 135.

12

Genesis One

The opening chapter of the Book of Genesis, so far as the subject of Christian evidences is concerned, is the most important chapter in the whole Bible. It begins with the recognition of the existence of God, and then describes His creation of the universe, with everything that is in it, including all forms of plants and animals, and, last of all, man. As one might well have expected of so significant a chapter, there have been many ways of understanding and interpreting its message down through the centuries.

In view of the many different interpretations by sincere Bible students, it would seem to be wise not to be dogmatic in insisting upon one's own views. There is an obvious danger in claiming that one's own interpretation is true, for it may not be true. It is unlikely that any person comprehends fully the message which God has so briefly sketched in this opening chapter of the Bible. The passing of time has demonstrated that some past interpretations have been very wrong and even ridiculous. This is not to say that the central message of the chapter cannot be comprehended, but it is to suggest that perhaps one ought to approach this brief description of the beginning of all things with some sense of his own limitations.

The significance of the chapter largely grows out of the fact that it deals with certain questions which man has long wished to understand more fully. These questions include, "Who is God?" "When did God create the universe?" "How was the creation accomplished?" "How long were the days mentioned in the chapter?" "At what place on the earth did the creation of man occur?" Of course, there are also many other questions. At this point it may be well to analyze the key verses of the chapter to determine just what meanings they do suggest. Since the chapter was written originally in Hebrew, it seems necessary to make some reference to several significant Hebrew words.

Analysis of the Text

Verse 1: "In the beginning . . . " (berḗ shîth). There is no indication when the beginning was. In fact, since this is a construct noun, as its relationship to the following words shows, it may even be translated: "In the beginning of. . . ." God's creating of the heavens and the earth.

Verse 2: "waste and void" (thoh̄û wābhōhû). It is interesting to note that there may have been a long period of time between God's initial creation and the forming of the earth into its present likeness. No one knows how long the earth was waste and void.

Verse 5: "day" (yôm). This word is just as ambiguous in Hebrew as it is in English. It can mean a twenty-four hour period, as it generally does when used with a definite number or when evening and morning are mentioned. It can also refer to a twelve-hour period, as when it is used in connection with night. It can also mean an indefinite period of time, such as an age or an era. In Genesis 2:4, the word "day" obviously includes everything mentioned in Genesis 1:1–2:3. Expressions like "unto this day" (Gen. 19:37, 38; 26:33) likely refer to the age in which the author lived rather than to a twenty-four hour period. "The day of the Lord," which occurs so often in the writings of the prophets, does not mean a twenty-four hour period, but rather a long period of punishment (Jer. 46:10). The fact that the sun and moon were put in their places to "rule the day and the night" (Gen. 1:16-18) only on the fourth day suggests that at least the first three days were somewhat different from our present days.

Verse 11: "After their kind" (min). This word does not have specific reference to the modern taxonomical system of classification into: species, genus, family, order, class, and phylum. It simply means that like begets like: dogs always have puppies; cats always have kittens; pear trees always bear pears. However, it might also be well to notice that in no case is the offspring *exactly* identical with the parent. There is some variation within the kind.

Verse 26: "Let us make man." Three verbs are used in the creation story which are translated into English as: create (bārā'), make (āsāh), and form (yāsar). All three words are applied to man: *make* is applied to him in Genesis 1:26; *create* is applied to him in Genesis 1:27; and *form* is applied to him in Genesis 2:7.

Verse 27: "In his own image" (selem). Man is made in the likeness of God, not physically, but spiritually. The idea is that man, unlike the animals of the earth, is an eternal spirit, a creature of choice, and possesses the ability to distinguish between right and wrong.

Verse 28: "replenish" (mālē'). The meaning of the word is simply "to fill" and does not imply the idea of doing something a second time.

Hypotheses of Creation

In order to explain the seemingly long period of time which the universe has existed, several hypotheses for the creation of the universe have been put forward. We mention some of the leading ones briefly, without wishing to be dogmatic concerning any of them. There are certain strong points in some of these theories, as well as certain weak points. In some instances, they overlap each other, or complement each other. Actually, we cannot know exactly how God created the earth or exactly when it was done, since man has no means of achieving certain knowledge of these matters. We have only the brief account which God has seen fit to give us.

There are five leading hypotheses which deserve our attention:

1. *Long Chaos:* This view holds that God created the universe "in the beginning" and that between verses one and two of Genesis 1 there is the possibility of an infinitely long period of time, during which "the earth was waste and void." During this period of chaos, it is suggested, some of the evidences of great age made their appearance on the earth.

2. *Creation-Ruination-Re-creation* (or Restitution or Gap Theory): This hypothesis holds that there has been a series of worlds such as our present one. Each time God has destroyed creation, allowed a period of chaos, and then recreated a new world. That the idea of destroying the world was not foreign to the mind of God is obvious in the story of the flood. (Gen. 6-8). This view provides the possibility that the earth is much older than the Adamic Age. It further opens the way for previous inhabitants in prior ages.

3. *Day-Age:* The idea in this theory is that the six "days" of the creation story really mean six long periods of time. Geology has vast periods of time in its terminology, such as Archeozoic, Proterozoic, Paleozoic, Mesozoic, and Cenozoic. These might correspond to the days of Genesis, according to this view.

4. *Pictorial Day:* Bernard Ramm's explanation of this theory is that it begins with this fact: "The main purpose of Genesis is theological and religious"—rather than scientific. Dr. Ramm continues, "The theological purpose of the passage [Genesis 1] is negative and positive. *Negatively,* it is a prohibition of idolatry. . . . *Positively,* the chapter teaches that the universe has its origin in God and reveals in a magnificent way God's power, God's spirituality, God's wisdom, and God's goodness. This is more effectively brought out by an absence of reference to all secondary causes."[1] Instead of a strict chronological explanation of the creation,

---

1. *The Christian View of Science and Scripture* (Grand Rapids, Mich.: Wm. B. Eerdmans Publishing Co., 1955), p. 219. Used with permission.

this theory holds that the six days are merely a device to present pictorially the creation story. Actually, the presentation is *topical* or *logical,* more than it is chronological.

5. *Literal:* This view holds that the six days of Genesis 1 are six literal twenty-four-hour days in which God created the universe in its entirety as it now appears. This is known as "fiat" creation. The "appearance" of great antiquity which the earth has is explained in terms of "pro-chronic or ideal time" by Philip Henry Gosse, as referred to by Ramm as follows:

> Every object of creation has two times. That which is before time or instantaneous in coming into existence is *pro-chronic.* That which consumes time is *dia-chronic.* All processes during the course of the world since its creation are *dia-chronic.* All things at the moment of creation were *pro-chronic.* Gosse also uses the terms real time and ideal time. At the moment of creation Adam's *real* time was zero—actually he did not exist till the moment of creation. His *ideal* time was, say for purposes of illustration, thirty years old. A tree in the garden of Eden would appear fifty years old (its ideal time) whereas it had just been created (its real time).[2]

In other words, when God created each object, He created it to appear as though it had passed through the usual stages of development. Thus the earth looked very old, at the moment of creation.

Conclusion

Rather than become dogmatically involved with any of the hypotheses of creation, it is well for the Christian to be aware of their possibilities and their limitations and to accept the Genesis account on faith. After all, it is the best account that man has of what happened "in the beginning." Dr. Wilbur Smith has summarized the message of Genesis 1 as follows:

---

2. Ramm, pp. 192-194, referring to Philip Henry Gosse, *Omphalos: An Attempt to Untie the Geological Knot* (1857).

"The first chapter of Genesis is placed at the beginning of our Bible, (1) to show mankind that the world in which he lives originally proceeded from the creative activity of God; (2) that God alone, the one true God, is the creator of the world; (3) that in creating the world He reveals Himself to be the eternal God, of omnipotence, omniscience, and infinite goodness; and (4) finally to inform man of the noble origin of the human species, and of the exalted dignity which must ever attach to the human race, because of the fact that man was originally made in the image of God."[3] We can never know exactly *when* God created our universe, nor exactly *how* he did it. We have the faith to believe that God had the power to create the universe instantaneously, by fiat creation, if that is the way he wished to do it. The exact details of creation are not revealed to us, but we can know God did it and that is the important thing.

---

3. *Therefore Stand,* pp. 309-310.

13

Age of the Earth

The age of the earth is one of the questions about which man has speculated longest and with greatest intensity of feeling. Many ideas have been advanced; many estimates have been given. Men of science have tended to speak of the earth as being very old, possibly several billions of years old, while religious leaders have traditionally spoken of the earth as being only a few thousand years old, possibly no more than six thousand. The differences between these two views are obviously great, affording unlimited opportunities for debates, which all too often have been accompanied by intense feelings. The average person, especially a young person, finds himself wondering which group is right.

A number of years ago, only a few days after our wedding, my wife and I spent a part of our honeymoon visiting the Grand Canyon of the Colorado River. One morning we found ourselves at Yavapai Point, looking out over the wide expanse of the Grand Canyon and listening to a United States National Parks geologist. This lecturer pointed to the black rocks at the bottom of the Grand Canyon and indicated that they were among the oldest rocks on earth. He estimated their age as a few billion years. Whether his estimate of their age was correct or not, he made a telling argument for their great age. He spoke of the fact that the entire region of that particular area of the United States was gradually rising. It had been rising over a long period of time, so long in fact that the Colorado River which ran directly through it in ancient times continued to run through the same path as the earth gradually rose. Hence, we have the unique situation of a river digging a channel more than five thousand feet deep, thus making the Grand Canyon. Had the area risen suddenly, he pointed out, the river would, of course, have flowed around the side of the large elevated dome, thus finding another path to the sea. Since the river continued to flow through its normal course, digging deeper and deeper into the earth's interior, there must have been the elapsing of a long period of time.

At a still earlier time I remember a vacation trip to California, with my family. Upon our return, we were passing through the mountains of Arizona, when my father pointed out, in a cut near the top of one of the mountains, that the mountain wall was made of shale. He explained that shale was a kind of rock that contains small sea shells and other evidences of having at one time been at the bottom of a great sea. As a child of twelve, I remember wondering just when the mountain tops of Arizona had been the bottom of some ancient sea.

At another time in our travels in the West, my family and I went through Carlsbad Caverns. The U.S. National Parks geologist who was our guide paused at one point to explain the supposed origin of the caverns. This mountain top cavern in New Mexico had resulted when an upheaval of earth settled back and then was eroded by the elements. Part of the mountain was composed of harder rocks, such as granite, intermixed with softer rock, such as limestone. During long periods of time the softer limestone had been worn away by the underground springs and rivers, leaving the huge cavern in which we then found ourselves, still surrounded by the harder stone that had not eroded away. At this point one needs to stop and remember what limestone is. It is formed on the bottom of lakes by the residue of the tiny animals that swim in the lakes. Their shells, skeletons, and bony structures gradually dissolve on the bottom of the lake and form limestone. If this geologist's theory of the origin of the Carlsbad Caverns is accurate, there must have been an ancient period in which there were lakes and ultimately limestone, followed by a great upheaval in which this softer rock was intermixed with the harder rocks as a great section of this continent was thrown up into new-made mountains. Obviously, this would indicate that the earth had been here a long time.

In the northwestern part of Yellowstone National Park in Wyoming, there is a phenomenon known as *Specimen Ridge.* At this location there is a two-thousand-foot stratigraphic section of a cliff on the side of Amethyst Mountain, in which eighteen successive petrified forests can be observed, one on top of the other. Each forest grew to maturity, was destroyed by a volcanic eruption, and eventually after the volcanic rock had eroded to rich soil, another forest grew.[1] This obviously required a vast amount of time.

Bishop Ussher's Calculations

Now, turn to the other side of the story. For several centuries readers of the King James Version of the Bible found the date 4004 B.C. printed on the first page of Genesis. The very manner in which the date was printed at the top of this first page of the Bible led many to believe that it was a part of the sacred text of the Scriptures themselves. Those who have respected the Bible, as a result, have thought that the God-given date for the beginning of creation and of the world is 4004 B.C. This would mean that the earth is something like six thousand years old, rather than several billion years old.

An explanation of the origin of the date 4004 B.C. is both important and necessary. An excellent explanation of this date is given by Dr. Bernard Ramm, a Bible-believing conservative:

> The date of 4004 B.C. was tagged on to the Bible well before the founding of modern geological theory. This

---

1. William John Miller, *An Introduction to Historical Geology,* 3rd ed. (New York: D. Van Nostrand Co., 1928), p. 335.

date goes back to the work of James Ussher (1581-1656), an Irishman and Archbishop of Armagh. Working with the genealogical tables in Genesis plus the other data of the Bible he deduced that there were about 4,036 years from the creation of the world to Christ. He followed through with a chronology for the entire Bible. These dates of Ussher have been almost canonized as they have been printed in English Bibles as part of the sacred page for centuries. Lightfoot (1602-1675), famed Hebraist of Cambridge, followed through with Ussher's work and figured out that creation took place the week of October 18 to 24, 4004 B.C., with Adam created on October 23 at 9:00 A.M. forty-fifth meridian time. Brewster sarcastically remarks: "Closer than this, as a cautious scholar, the Vice-Chancellor of Cambridge University did not venture to commit himself."[2]

Genealogy or Chronology?

Bishop Ussher arrived at his figure of 4004 B.C. by calculating the ages mentioned in the genealogies which are occasionally included in the text of the Scriptures. It should be pointed out that it is impossible to get an exact date by this method, since there are periods of Bible history, such as the period of the Judges, during which no one was on the throne and there are other periods when two men served at the same time. At best, there are certain gaps in this method of estimating the age of the earth.

However, there is a far more significant consideration. Are the genealogies of the Bible meant to be chronologies? Dr. J. D. Thomas has this rather comprehensive statement on this entire subject:

> Ussher's computation is discounted today by all scholars who have made a study of this matter because it is known that he made mistakes; because it is questionable which text may be the correct one for these portions of the Old Testament; and especially because there is good evidence

---

2. *The Christian View of Science and Scripture* p. 174, and quoting E. T. Brewster, *Creation: A History of Non-Evolutionary Theories* (1927), p. 109.

that the genealogical list of the patriarchs were not intended to be chronologically complete; and further, because there would be very significant questions raised by the overlapping of the lives of certain of the Old Testament patriarchs if Ussher's date be correct. . . . *Young's Analytical Concordance,* in the article on "Creation" quotes Doctor Hales as listing one hundred and forty different actual dates varying from 6984 B.C. to 3616 B.C. as the date for Adam. . . . All Bible chronologies come together and agree in a general way from Abraham's day on down to the present time. . . . Apparently a serious mistake that some conservatives have made in these matters in the past is to assume that the genealogy, or list of ancestors, from Adam to Abraham was also to be considered as an exact chronology, or exact dating of these men and their lives "end to end." A genealogy is purposed to show the line through which the descent comes; a chronology is purposed to show the exact lengths of time covered. What we have in the Bible is only a genealogy, and there is no evidence that it was intended to be an exact chronology.[3]

Byron C. Nelson also discussed the question of whether the Biblical genealogies were meant to be chronologies:

The genealogies of Scripture must be regarded as abridged. God had no intention that they should be used for the construction of a chronology. So far as the Bible is concerned, the date of the creation of Adam and Eve may be many times earlier than Ussher supposed. While it is pure speculation at present to say that the human race is a hundred thousand years old, there is nothing in Scripture which forbids such an assumption. No proved or imagined antiquity of man can be too great to be accepted by Christians, since no fundamental doctrine is in any way involved.[4]

While this appears to me to be a vast overstatement of the case, allowing an unreasonably large expansion of the time

---

3. *Facts and Faith,* Vol. I, *Reason, Science and Faith* (Abilene, Texas: Biblical Research Press, 1965), pp. 166-167.

4. *Before Abraham* (Minneapolis, Minn.: Augsburg Publishing House, 1948), p. 16.

covered in Biblical history, it is worthy of some consideration.

Dr. John W. Klotz also discusses the abridgment of genealogies:

> However, there is some evidence that these may not be
> simple father-and-son relationships. We know that abridg-
> ment of genealogies is very common in Scripture and may
> almost be said to be the rule. Time after time we find the
> term *son* used where clearly the term means *descendant,*
> not *son.* For instance, in the very first verse of Matthew's
> Gospel, Christ is called "the Son of David, the Son of
> Abraham." In the same chapter in verse 8 three names are
> omitted between Joram and Ozias (Uzziah).

Old Testament	Matthew
Joram (II Kings 8:24)	Joram (Matt. 1:8)
Ahaziah (II Kings 8:24)	
Joash (II Kings 11:2)	
Amaziah (II Kings 14:1)	
Uzziah (II Chron. 26:1)	Ozias (Matt. 1:8)
Again, in Matt. 1:11 Jehoiakim is omitted.	
Josiah (II Kings 22:1)	Josias [Matt. 1:11]
Jehoiakim (II Kings 23:34)	
Jehoiachin (II Kings 24:6)	Jechonias [Greek form of Jehoiachin] (Matt. 1:11)

> It may be helpful to consider the purpose of the
> genealogical tables in Genesis. Certainly the purpose was
> not to give us an exact chronological account of those
> times, for if that were the case, there would be no
> omissions. The Holy Spirit would not have permitted
> Moses to omit any names if that had been His purpose. It
> seems rather that God wanted to give us the names of the
> most important men who lived between Adam and Abra-
> ham and wanted to give us a brief account of what
> occurred in that period. It is also evident that the Lord
> wanted to show us how the earth was populated in keep-
> ing with His command (Gen. 1:28 and Gen. 9:1). By the
> time of the Flood the human race had spread over much

of the face of the earth, and it is the purpose of Genesis 5 to show how this spread was accomplished. In Genesis 11 the emphasis is on the spread of the descendants of Shem after the Flood. But why should God have included the ages of these patriarchs? Chiefly to show how the human race could have increased in numbers so rapidly. Because these men attained such great ages, they were able to beget large numbers of sons and daughters. In this way, the world was populated rather quickly.[5]

Modern Methods of Estimating the Earth's Antiquity

Dr. Frederick E. Zeuner listed seven ways that the earth and various objects on the earth are dated. The following is a summary of his introductory list of these geochronological methods of dating:

(1) *Tree ring analysis,* covering the past three thousand years;

(2) *Varved clay analysis,* covering a period of about fifteen thousand years;

(3) *Radio-carbon dating,* covering a period of about thirty thousand years;

(4) *"Per cent of equilibrium method"* (a form of radium dating), covering about three hundred thousand years;

(5) *Solar radiation,* covering approximately one million years;

(6) *Typical geological methods* (sedimentation, denudation, erosion, weathering, and chemical changes) applicable to all periods; and

(7) *Uranium and radio-active methods,* with a range of some three billion years.[6]

Within the past score of years the methods of dating very old objects by radioactivity have been refined greatly. In the late 1950's the "carbon-14 process" was widely used and was

5. From *Genes, Genesis, and Evolution* by John W. Klotz. (St. Louis: Concordia Publishing House, 1955, 1970), pp. 92-93, 95. Used with permission.

6. *Dating the Past, An Introduction to Geochronology,* 4th ed., rev. (London: Methuen & Co. Ltd., 1958), pp. 4-5.

considered to be quite dependable for periods up to thirty
thousand years. By comparing certain objects which could be
dated because of their historical setting with the carbon-14
method, it was found that this method was accurate within a
plus or minus 10 percent range. Objects from the pyramids
which could be dated by both methods were quite helpful in
establishing the validity of this method of dating.

Linen wrappings from the Dead Sea scrolls also indicated
that they were more than nineteen hundred years old. Lotus
seeds, still capable of sprouting, were found twenty feet
below ground near Tokyo, Japan. They showed an age of
three thousand years by the carbon-14 process. This same
method of dating has indicated that Stonehenge in England
dates back to about 1800 B.C., Crater Lake in Oregon to
about 4500 B.C., woven sagebrush sandles found in Oregon
to about 7,000 B.C., and an ancient Egyptian wooden boat
to about 1850 B.C. Tests on some of the giant redwood
trees in California indicated that they were about twenty-
seven hundred years old, while the tree-ring count indicated
that they dated back about twenty-nine hundred years.[7]

A later development has been the "potassium-argon
method" and although this involves a far more intricate
process, some scientists believe that it is a dependable means
of measuring the age of objects that are at least a few million
years old. It was through this method that the bones found
by Dr. and Mrs. Louis S. B. Leakey, in the Olduvai Gorge in
Tanganyika, East Africa, and named Zinjanthropus, were
considered to be 1,750,000 years old.[8]

After carefully examining the data produced by the radiocarbon and potassium-argon methods of dating, Dr. Robert
L. Whitelaw points out some weaknesses in these methods:

> Of the various "clocks" proposed for dating events in
> geological history, the two in principal favor today are

---

7. Lyman Briggs and Kenneth Weaver, "How Old Is It?," *National Geographic* (Aug., 1958), pp. 235-255.
8. Lewis S. B. Leakey, "Exploring 1,750,000 Years Into the Past," *National Geographic* (Oct., 1961), pp. 564-588

radiocarbon, for events in the biosphere, and potassium-argon, for events in the lithosphere.

The C-14 or radiocarbon clock presumes to date the death of any biological specimen, animal or vegetable, with reasonable accuracy up to six or eight half-lives of carbon-14 (about 45,000 years). It has been in extensive use since 1950 by leading universities of the world, as witness the exhaustive listings of almost 10,000 dates in the annual journal, *Radiocarbon*. . . .

The potassium-argon clock presumes to date entrapment of any tiny sample of potassium-bearing rock, based upon assumptions and methods described earlier, and generally yields dates between 1 and 10 billion.

Both clocks are *absolutely* dependent upon accurate knowledge of a tiny constituent of the earth's atmosphere at the time of the event being dated. The radiocarbon clock . . . *assumes* that the C-14 concentration throughout the living world was the same at the death of the specimen as it is today.

This assumption is based on two prior assumptions: (a) that the production rate of C-14 in the outer atmosphere had long before approached equilibrium with the decay rate, i.e., that "creation," if it occurred at all, was long before living matter; and (b) that no cosmic events occurred in the last 45,000 years that could possibly change the C-14 production rate or decay rate.[9]

This study would seem to question the reliability of both these methods of dating, at least to some degree.

Dr. Delbert Eggenberger also writes concerning the age of the earth:

The oldest of the rocks of the earth's crust is the uranite of Manitoba, which dates 2.4 billion years ago. An analysis of the lead isotopes leads to a figure of 3.5 billion years. The rate of disintegration of uranium-235 suggests a date of several billion years. Meteorites are dated five billion years old. Star clusters are dated three billion years old. Recent work with the 200-inch telescope on

9. "Radiocarbon and Potassium-Argon Dating in the Light of New Discoveries in Cosmic Rays," *Creation Research Society, 1969 Annual* (June, 1969), p. 71.

Mt. Palomar suggests 5.5 billion years as the absolute maximum for the age of the earth.[10]

Concerning the age of the earth's rocks, Dr. Edwin Gedney gives us these additional words:

Studies of the oldest known rocks by radioactivity estimates indicate an age of about 2,200,000,000 years with other more recent rocks showing proportionately smaller figures. The processes by which these ages are arrived at are generally regarded by physicists, chemists, and geologists as dependable and the figures acceptable as reasonable approximations of the general correct magnitude.[11]

Dr. Peter W. Stoner, drawing upon the field of astronomy, has also indicated the earth's great age:

Astronomy has thus indicated the age of the whole physical universe, at least in its present state, as something between 2 and 10 billion years. . . .

If the ultimate age of the earth, the moon, the meteorites, the galaxies, and, in fact, all known astronomical objects (at least in their present form) is between 2 and 10 billion years, or if the ultimate age limit is any other finite period of time, we are led to conclude that the universe was either created from nothing or that its state of existence was very drastically changed at a limited period of time in the past. Genesis states a creation of the universe. It does not state when or how that creation took place. Astronomy not only does not contradict a creation but gives all the evidence cited above that such a creative act did take place.[12]

Conclusion

The message of this chapter is well summarized in a statement from Dr. Klotz:

10. "Methods of Dating the Earth and the Universe," *Journal of the American Scientific Affiliation* (March, 1951), pp. 1-3.

11. "Geology," *Modern Science and Christian Faith: A Symposium on the Relationship of the Bible to Modern Science,* by members of The American Scientific Affiliation (Chicago: Scripture Press, 1950), p. 27.

12. "Astronomy," *Modern Science and Christian Faith,* pp. 16, 17.

What shall we say, then, about the age of the earth? We shall have to say that Scripture gives us no exact dates before the time of Abraham. It is impossible to give an exact date for Creation, and we cannot say on the basis of Scripture how old the earth is. God simply did not feel that it was necessary for us to know its exact age. Apparently the age of the earth has no bearing on our salvation. This is not to be regarded as a plea for the acceptance of the figures of some geologists and evolutionists: it is merely a statement that on the basis of Scripture we cannot establish definitely how old the earth is.[13]

---

13. *Genes, Genesis, and Evolution,* p. 96.

14

History of Man

Questions constantly arise about how long man has been on the earth. Men of both science and religion are agreed that man's arrival on the earth has been relatively recent. The scientists who believe that the earth is four or five billion years old are quick to say that man has been on the earth only one or two million years. The historian, from his study of the record that man has left behind him, discovers that man's stay on the earth has been far briefer than that. In fact, the historian finds himself in rather large agreement with the Biblical account of man's span upon the earth. But just how do men arrive at these differing views of man's antiquity? There are essentially two approaches: an analysis of certain bone fragments found in various parts of the world by the archaeologists and anthropologists; and the historical record that man has left of himself in various parts of the world.

Archaeology

During the last century a number of fossil remains have been discovered in various parts of the world which appear to be fragmentary remains of man-like creatures. Among these the Neanderthal Man is represented by a group of fossils found in Germany in 1856. These remains are thought by some to go back to a period between 115,000 and 200,000 years ago. There are more of these fossils than of any other group, possibly eighty to ninety different fossils; however, many of these specimens consist of only a few fragments.

These fossils are classified as relatively recent, dating back only to the Old Stone Age.

Some fragmentary bones were discovered by a Dutch army physician by the name of DuBois in Java in 1890. These remains are known as *Pithecanthropus erectus* and are claimed to have been the remains of man-like creatures who lived 500,000 years ago. The Heidelberg Man was discovered in 1907 near the city for which it was named. This fossil consists of only a lower jaw with most of the teeth intact. It is thought by some to date back some 435,000 years.

In 1912 two Englishmen discovered the Piltdown Man in a gravel pit in the south of England. The bones were variously estimated by geologists and anthropologists at from two hundred thousand to one million years old. However, it was later discovered that these fossils were a complete hoax, a plant by some unknown joker. It is now generally believed that the lower jaw and canine tooth are those of an anthropoid ape, deliberately altered so as to resemble a fossil.

In 1922 a number of fossils were found near Peking, China, and these fragmentary remains have become known as Peking Man, or *Sinanthropus*. It is claimed that these remains are two hundred thousand years old. The Folsom Man found near Lubbock, Texas, is thought to be some ten thousand years old and is one of the relatively few early man-like remains to be found in North America.

In 1960, Dr. and Mrs. Louis S. B. Leakey found the remains of what they have called a man-like creature which they named *Zinjanthropus,* as they excavated in Olduvai Gorge in Tanganyika, East Africa. Drs. Garniss Curtis and Jack Evernden of the University of California dated these remains as being 1,750,000 years old. They used the modern potassium-argon technique to find that volcanic ash or tuff found in the same gravel pit where *Zinjanthropus* was discovered dates back one and three-quarter million years. Accordingly, they assumed that these remains are from that same period of time.

The study of primitive man is a science of very recent

origin, dating back hardly more than a century. The relatively meager fossil finds have led to several widely divergent theories about how early man came to be and how he spread over the earth. There are many questions yet to be answered before any definitive conclusions can be drawn. The problem of dating primitive man is made more difficult because of the fact that primitive peoples, much like some of those mentioned above, are still living in the wild and far-off places of the world today. Among these are the Bushmen of South Africa and the dark-skinned, Stone Age hunters of the Out-Back in Australia.

The Historical Period

Dr. J. D. Thomas gives an unusually comprehensive, yet brief, survey of the historical period of man's existence upon the earth. His summary follows:

> What we know today in scholarly circles as "the historical period" of man goes back only to about 5000 to 7000 B.C., as scientists accept it. Indeed, we are highly uncertain about any civilization that would date much older than around 5000 to 6000 B.C. Our first cities that we know anything about date to around 5000 B.C., ancient Jericho of Old Testament fame being the oldest city that we know of anywhere at the present time. About this time people quit living in caves. . . . Of course, in thinking about cave men and cave life, we should realize that this is still going on in some places of the world, notably among the Australian Aborigines. . . .
>
> Another evidence of the recency of man is that the first writing of which we know began in about 3200 B.C. This is pictographic writing or what we commonly think of as hieroglyphics. . . . Later on cuneiform writing was invented and also the use of syllabic writing. . . . Alphabetic writing, so far as we can now tell, dates somewhere between 1500 to 1800 or 1900 B.C. . . . What all of this means is that between 3200 B.C. and about 1700 B.C. (in round numbers), a period of 1500 years, man learned how to write. . . . It is accepted that human nature (if it has ever changed) does not change fast; and admittedly

there has been no change in the last 7000 years in human capability, even on the part of those who believe that evolution has occurred. . . . However, if man, intelligent as he is today, has been on earth for a hundred thousand or two hundred thousand or a million or two million years, why do all of the evidences of civilization and of what we call a genuinely historical period arise suddenly and as late as 5000 or 6000 B.C.? What has this intelligent man been doing all of these thousands of years, if he has been here? . . . As far as tools are concerned, 5000 B.C. is in the late stone age, but copper was invented as usable for tools soon after this and bronze next came into use. The bronze age reached down to 1200 B.C. when iron came in. . . . From this we can see that the best evidence offered concerning ancient human remains is based on highly tentative dating.[1]

Conclusion

Admittedly, the two areas from which we find information about man's existence on earth are difficult to interpret and to relate one to the other. If man has been on the earth as long as Dr. Lewis S. B. Leakey thinks that he has, some 1,750,000 years, one wonders what he has been doing all of this time, since his historical record goes back only some seven to nine thousand years. To put it another way, man's historical record goes back only about one-half of 1 percent of the alleged time that Dr. Leakey thinks that man-like creatures have been on the earth. Again we ask, "What has man been doing all of this time if he really has been here?"

---

1. *Facts and Faith,* I, 172-174.

15

Theory of Evolution

Contrary to popular assumption, there is not just one way of looking at organic evolution. Actually, there are many theories, almost as many theories as there are scientists discussing the subject. The *Encyclopedia Britannica* lists twenty-two different theories of evolution. Among these are the following, which seem most significant for our present study:

1. *Atheistic evolution.* This theory holds that there is no God and that the natural universe and its laws originated by chance. This is a purely mechanistic outlook. It appeals to many because it eliminates the necessity of a God who requires the submission of man's will.

2. *Deistic evolution.* This theory holds that the processes of evolution are controlled by a great, impersonal Mind, one who is concerned only with events, but is not interested in individuals.

3. *Theistic evolution.* This theory holds that God personally guides the evolutionary processes as, for example, a chess player moves his chess men. Usually the theistic evolutionist identifies this God with the God of the Bible.

The word *evolution* is generally understood to refer to the hypothesis or theory that all life on earth originated from non-living matter and that all forms of life on the earth today came from some original form of life by a connected series of changes, which at every point were only natural, and are therefore explainable by science. Vast expanses of time are envisioned during which these changes came about. Most evolutionists insist that there is no mind behind or at work in

119

the universe and that there is no power active in the history of life, other than that which is purely mechanical and inherent in nature as we now know it. In defining the term *evolution,* we do not mean simply a change in living forms, since these are recognized by all, but rather the idea that all life on earth today came from some original form of life by a connected series of changes.

In his *Introduction to Evolution,* Paul Amos Moody, himself an evolutionist, defines evolution in these words:

> For our purposes we may define organic evolution as the theory that plants and animals now living are the modified descendants of somewhat different plants and animals that lived in times past. These ancestors, in their turn, are thought of as being the descendants of predecessors that differed from them, and so on, step by step, back to a beginning shrouded in mystery.[1]

With the characteristic confidence and enthusiasm of evolutionists generally, Moody had said in the preface of his book:

> Organic evolution is the greatest general principle in biology. Its implications extend far beyond the confines of that science, ramifying into all phases of human life and activity. Accordingly, an understanding of evolution should be part of the intellectual equipment of all educated persons.[2]

History of Evolutionary Thought

Before Charles Darwin published his *Origin of Species* in 1859, writers on the subject of anatomy often interspersed praises of the Creator with their descriptions of life. Books describing the marvels of nature often had what might be considered a religious tone. After Darwin, such passages of praise to the Creator God slipped completely out of the text books. Charles Darwin and Thomas Huxley, although they did not establish any consistent theory as to how evolution

---

1. Moody, pp. 1-2.
2. Moody, p. ix.

works, popularized the idea that "natural selection and the survival of the fittest" explains modern day life. Darwin's theory of "natural selection" was rapidly and widely accepted, though it has since been greatly modified and is not now generally accepted in the same form as originally suggested. Hugo de Vries, the Dutch botanist, pointed out that the main weakness of natural selection is that "natural selection may explain the survival of the fittest, but it cannot explain the arrival of the fittest." Of course, the real test of the evolutionary hypothesis is some explanation of how the various forms of life began.

Along the evolutionary road there came the announcement of the immediately popular theory of Lamarck, known as "the inheritance of acquired characteristics." This is the theory that environment causes effects which are passed on to offspring. As examples of the inheritance of acquired characteristics, Lamarck theorized that the stretching of the giraffe for foliage resulted in the development of its long neck. Similarly, snakes at one time were lizard-like, but wore off their original legs when they developed the habit of crawling through holes to escape danger. This theory is no longer held, because it has not stood the test of scientific investigation. Lamarck also advocated the idea that a trait possessed but not used by the immediate ancestors atrophies through disuse and is not passed on to offspring. This theory, too, has been rather generally abandoned. In one study twenty-two generations of rats had their tails cut off soon after birth. After all this passage of time each new generation of rats was still born with tails.

Thomas D. S. Key points out that:

> As biologists became more aware of laws of heredity, it became progressively evident that species must do more than simply "improve" by a mere selection of the fit. It was discovered that in order to acquire new organs a species must acquire new genes (hereditary determiners inside each cell). How could this happen in the light of the hereditary law that "like begets like?" Hugo de Vries

. . . noted what appeared to be rare but striking exceptions to the "like begets like" law. . . . [He thought that] evolution occurs, not gradually as Darwin believed, but visibly and suddenly in great jumps. Many genuine examples of hereditary changes have since been found on the gene level, and are known variously as saltations, mutations, mutants, sports, and "freaks."

. . . Although mutationists could rally such noteworthy examples as the Shetland pony, Kentucky wonder bean, change in eye color in the fruit fly . . . and others, they were faced with a growing number of insistent problems such as the following: (1) the number of original mutations of all kinds in extremely low; (2) beneficial mutations are far less common than neutral, harmful, or fatal ones; and (3) mutations have never been observed to produce new organs.[3]

Key gives an excellent summary of the generally accepted view of modern science:

. . . modern Western biologists as a whole believe something like the following regarding the manner of evolution:

(1) Genetic recombination occurs whenever an egg is fertilized, shuffling traits already in existence.

(2) Random mutations arise spontaneously from time to time that add new hereditary traits to the species. Some of these are fatal, many are harmful, and many are merely neutral—that is, neither beneficial nor harmful— and a very few of all mutations are beneficial. Most are somewhat similar to the normal (or "wild type"), though some may be radical departures from the normal.

(3) Natural selection tends to eliminate those genetic recombinations and random mutations that do not adjust to environmental demands, and to favor reproduction of those which do fit environmental demands. Thus, in time a population shift will be brought about. Natural selection may not be limited to violent struggles between organisms, as supposed by many of Darwin's early disciples, but often includes adaptability to changing physical factors such as drought, cold weather, etc.

---

3. "The Influence of Darwin on Biology," in *Evolution and Christian Thought Today,* ed. Russell L. Mixter, pp. 25-26.

(4) Speciation occurs when the traits of a population shift so far from the original ones that reproduction can no longer take place between earlier and later varieties, or when anatomical and other differences are pronounced.

Most modern creationists would agree with each of the above factors, but would insist that while species can lose some traits and gain new ones, the fluctuations in any genus or family are extremely limited. A creationist can consider the foregoing four points as the Creator's means of giving to each organism a limited ability to adapt to changing environments.[4]

Summary

Through the centuries man has been curious concerning the origin of life in general and the origin of specific varieties of life in particular. There are two opposite views. During the past century there has been a general acceptance of the idea that all life had a chance origin in the dim, distant, prehistoric past. The older, more traditional view holds that at a definite time in the past God created the universe and a number of different forms of life. This is the view of "fiat creation," or instantaneous creation, by the miraculous power of God. Between these two poles, there are certain other modifications and gradations of each position. The thoughtful student seeks to understand each position and to evaluate each according to the evidence available.

---

4. Key, p. 27.

16

Thermodynamics

The theory of evolution holds the view that there is a gradual development from lower and simpler forms of life to higher and more sophisticated forms of life. It is believed that, even though the process is extremely slow, living things are constantly improving as life moves up the evolutionary ladder. From the simple amoeba, or some similar form, life has progressed, according to the evolutionary view, up to modern man. Progress and improvement are essential to the evolutionary theory. The evolutionary view is operative primarily in the realm of living things—the realm of biology.

There are certain phenomena in the related realm of physics, which have some implications for the realm of biology. Instead of everything getting better and better as time passes, it appears that among the physical objects of the universe, just the reverse is true. Among the most generally accepted principles or laws in the realm of physics are the two laws that have to do with thermodynamics. These, it would seem, have certain interesting implications concerning the evolutionary hypothesis.[1]

Dr. Henry M. Morris, in discussing the two primary energy laws, speaks of their general acceptance and of their fundamental nature:

---

1. Some conservative Christian scientists discount the validity of the argument against evolution from the laws of thermodynamics, on the ground that our system is not a closed system. Others hold that when the sun is included, our universe is a closed system. We leave the reader to evaluate these diverse points of view.

This powerful scientific concept of energy is embodied in two great laws, which are the two most basic, universal, and important laws of all science. They are known as the first and second laws of thermodynamics. The name arises from the fact that, historically, they were first discovered and proved in the study of thermodynamics, the science of heat power, but their applicability has since been proved to extend to literally every branch of human scientific knowledge. The great Harvard physicist, P. W. Bridgman, says, for example: "The two laws of thermodynamics are, I suppose, accepted by physicists as perhaps the most secure generalizations from experience that we have. The physicist does not hesitate to apply the two laws to any concrete situation in the confidence that nature will not let him down."[2]

Dr. Morris then explains in some detail the meaning of the first law of thermodynamics:

The first law of thermodynamics is also known as the law of energy conservation and states that although energy can change forms it cannot be either created or destroyed and therefore the sum total of energy remains constant. Energy can appear in many forms, including light, heat, sound, pressure, electricity, chemical energy, mechanical energy, nuclear energy, etc., and all of these are, under the proper conditions, interchangeable. Numerical conversion factors are known, in most cases, to express the transformation of energy from one form into another. And it is significant that all real processes in nature, as well as those invented by man, necessarily involve the utilization and transformation of energy, in order to accomplish the work involved in the processes.

But as these interchanges take place, this law insists that the total amount of energy put into the system must equal the total taken out. None of it is destroyed, nor is any new energy created in the process. This is true in any small system or process and must therefore be true for any combination of such systems, and is true for the universe as a whole. Therefore, no energy is now being

2. Henry M. Morris, *Studies in the Bible and Science,* p. 48, and quoting P. W. Bridgman, "Reflections on Thermodynamics," *American Scientist* (October, 1953), 549.

created or destroyed anywhere in the universe, so far as science can know. And since matter itself is merely one form of energy, this means that creation is not taking place now at all.

This in turn leads to the conclusion that when energy was originally created the processes of creation must have been entirely different than those now being observed in the universe and that, therefore, the Creation itself cannot be studied at all by means of modern science; revelation is required.[3]

It is interesting to note that in the first chapter of Genesis, following the familiar Biblical account of creation, we find the following statement: "And the heavens and the earth were finished, and all the host of them. And on the seventh day God finished his work which he had made; and he rested on the seventh day from all his work which he had made" (Gen. 2:1-2). The Bible declares that the creation process was the insertion of creative energy from outside our universe. This was different from the present order of things which we now can observe and was completed at the time of God's creative acts. This would seem to be quite consistent with the first law of thermodynamics.

Dr. Morris turns his attention next to an explanation of the second law of thermodynamics:

> The second law of thermodynamics states that in any real process or system in which energy is being transformed into other forms, at least some of it is transformed into heat energy which cannot be converted back into other useful forms. That is, although none of the energy is destroyed, some of it deteriorates and becomes less useful and available for work than it was at the beginning of the process. In a more general sense, this law expresses the fact that in any closed system there must always be a decrease of order or organization, unless external energy or intelligence is applied to counteract this trend.
>
> Again, since the universe as a whole can be considered as an aggregation of finite systems, this law implies that

---

3. Morris, pp. 48-49.

there is a continual decrease of useful energy for performing the work of running the universe or, in other terms, that there is a continual increase of disorder in the universe. The universe is therefore growing old, wearing out, running down, due ultimately to burn itself out when all of its useful energy is converted to unavailable heat energy and the entire universe reaches a constant, uniform, low temperature, and ceases all its motions.[4]

As a matter of comparison, it is interesting at this point to remember the words of the apostle Peter concerning the termination of the earth's existence:

The Lord is not slack concerning his promise, as some count slackness; but is longsuffering to you-ward, not wishing that any should perish, but that all should come to repentance. But the day of the Lord will come as a thief; in the which the heavens shall pass away with a great noise, and the elements shall be dissolved with fervent heat, and the earth and the works that are therein shall be burned up. Seeing that these things are thus all to be dissolved, what manner of persons ought ye to be in all holy living and godliness, looking for and earnestly desiring the coming of the day of God, by reason of which the heavens being on fire shall be dissolved, and the elements shall melt with fervent heat? But according to his promise, we look for new heavens and a new earth, wherein dwelleth righteousness (II Pet. 3:9-13).

Dr. R. B. Lindsay further explained the effect of the second law of thermodynamics:

On this interpretation, the meaning of the second law of thermodynamics, the law of increasing entropy, is now clear. In any naturally occurring process, the tendency is for all systems to proceed from order to disorder. . . . From this point of view, the trend from order to disorder with production of entropy is inexorable. The second law always wins in the end.[5]

---

4. Morris, pp. 49-50.
5. R. B. Lindsay, "Entrophy Consumption and Values in Physical Science," *American Scientist,* 47:382(September, 1959).

Dr. John W. Klotz points up the conflict between the process of deterioration, as evidenced in the second law of thermodynamics, and the theory of evolution which claims that things are going toward a more orderly state.

> Another principle to be considered in this connection is the second law of thermodynamics, a physical principle which states that there is a continual tendency toward greater randomness. Evolution suggests that in the biological world the very opposite is true and that instead of a tendency toward greater randomness there is a tendency toward a higher degree of organization. . . . It would be very unusual for the biological world to follow a principle entirely different from that followed by the inorganic world.[6]

Dr. Morris also draws a sharp contrast between the supposed direction of movement in the realm of biology and the known direction of movement in the real of physics:

> And these two laws are fundamentally and basically in opposition to the entire philosophy of evolution. Evolution says that present processes are the same as those by which the universe came into existence and is thus still coming into existence. But the first law of thermodynamics says that no energy (and this includes everything) is now coming into existence. No energy is being either created or destroyed.
> Furthermore, evolution says that there is a universal law whereby things tend to become progressively more organized and more complex. The non-living becomes life; elementary particles become atoms and atoms become molecules; simple life forms develop into complex animals, beasts evolve into men.[7]

Summary

While not a conclusive argument against evolution, the behavior of the physical elements of the universe, as stated in

---

6. *Genes, Genesis, and Evolution*, p. 546.
7. Morris, pp. 145-146.

the first and second laws of thermodynamics, would seem to be in direct contrast to the development claimed by the evolutionists in the realm of living things. Dr. Van Rensselaer Potter, in terms which the average man can understand, indicates the downward direction in which things normally move.

> Man has long been aware that his world has a tendency to fall apart. Tools wear out, fishing nets need repair, roofs leak, iron rusts, wood decays, loved ones sicken and die, relatives quarrel, and nations make war. . . . We instinctively resent the decay of orderly systems such as the living organism and work to restore such systems to their former or even a higher level of organization.[8]

In a world where the general trend seems to be toward falling apart, wearing out, and fading away, it does seem that the evolutionist has a heavy burden of proof upon his shoulders to show that in one large segment of the scientific realm all movement is in the opposite direction.

------

8. Van Rensselaer Potter, "Society and Science," *Science,* Vol. 146 (November 20, 1964), 1018.

17

Fixity of Species

During the creation-evolution debates that were so wide-spread in the first quarter of the century, one of the most important conflicts centered around the problem of "fixity of species." At that time it was generally assumed that "kind" in Genesis 1 and "species" in biology were synonymous; therefore, since Genesis implied that kinds were stable units, many Christians became ardent defenders of the fixity of species. The theory of evolution holds that life has progressed from the single celled amoeba, or some similar form, through the various levels to the highest and most sophisticated forms. It holds that there has been vast, upward movement and therefore contradicts the idea of "fixity of species." On the other hand, creationists hold with Genesis that the various forms of life have stayed within relatively limited boundaries, each producing after its own "kind."

Perhaps it would be of value at this point to review the taxonomical divisions of the plant and animal world. Dr. John W. Klotz gives this brief summary of the system now generally used by scientists throughout the world:

> The living world is divided, first of all, into two kingdoms, the plant kingdom and the animal kingdom. These are then divided into phyla. Most taxonomists classify the plant kingdom into four phyla and the animal kingdom into some twenty phyla. The *phyla* [italics here and following are inserted] are further divided into *classes;* the classes into *orders;* the orders into *families;* the families into *genera;* and the genera into *species.*[1]

---

1. *Genes, Genesis, and Evolution,* p. 121.

Our first concern is to know exactly what is meant by species. Dr. Irving W. Knobloch provides this definition of a species:

> A species may be considered as a large or small population of individuals having so many genes in common that their variation pattern is slight when compared to the variation pattern of the population of a related species.[2]

Dr. Gerald T. Den Hartog makes the following observations concerning species:

> A plant species has been defined by the French botanist de Jussieu as "the perennial succession of similar individuals perpetuated by generation." . . . By natural selection and human selection progress has been made. . . . There is reason to believe that this progress will continue in the future. However—and this is the great point to be stressed—basically the plant species remain the same all through the ages, regardless of selective processes, changes in climate and environment, or persistent and widespread attacks by biological enemies. The Creator's mandate in Genesis 1 is being carried out to this very day.
>
> A striking illustration of the persistency of plant species is provided by the archaeological finds of wheat seed and other plant products that correspond to our present-day species and that have remained relatively unchanged over thousands of years. . . .
>
> It is true, mutations (alterations) occur in plant life, though with extreme infrequency—chromosomal mutations and gene mutations. But also these leave the species itself intact. . . . Gene mutations also occur. . . . Muller studied the equivalent of some one thousand or more generations of the fruit fly . . . and reports that the mutated genes are all deleterious or at best similar in effect to the original gene complex. . . . All these and similar studies indicated that there was no change in the species.[3]

2. Knobloch, "The Role of Hybridization in Evolution," *Evolution and Christian Thought Today,* ed. Mixter, p. 94.

3. "Footsteps of God in the Plant World," *The Evidence of God in an Expanding Universe,* ed. Monsma, pp. 103-104.

Dr. Klotz also writes concerning the definition of species and the question of change:

> It is generally agreed that two forms belong to the same species if they can interbreed and produce fertile offspring. If we accept this definition, we shall have to admit that new species have arisen, both out in nature and in the laboratory. However, it should be noted that Genesis does not use the term "species." The Hebrew word *"min"* is best translated "kind." It is not an exact equivalent of the term "species." While new species can arise, new "kinds" cannot.[4]

Dr. Knobloch freely admits changes of species, but argues that they are well within the range of the word "kind" of Genesis 1:

> That changes in species are taking place today by hybridization and other methods, no one can doubt. This poses a serious question for those who have been taught that the Bible rules out changes. It is my opinion that the Bible is not at all specific on this point. "Kinds" still reproduce after their kind, but children never look exactly like their parents. Granted that man *was* created, mutations and crossings have produced the three races and the multitude of groups within those races. Conservative Christians can believe in the divine creation of the major groups of organisms and still be modern enough to believe in the natural laws of change.[5]

Dr. Wilbert Rusch of the Creation Research Society, a group made up of several hundred scientifically trained men who hold the creationist view of the origin of life, includes the following in an article:

> Recently the French biologist, Prof. Louis Bounoure, quoted Yves Delage, a late Sorbonne professor of zoology, as saying: "I readily admit that no species has ever been known to engender another, and that there is no absolutely definite evidence that such a thing has ever taken

---

4. Klotz, p. 81
5. Mixter, p. 103.

place. Nonetheless, I *believe* evolution to be just as certain as if it had been objectively proved." Incidentally, Bounoure comments: "In short what science asks of us here is an act of faith, and it is in fact under the guise of a sort of revealed truth that the idea of evolution is generally put forward."[6]

Transitional Forms

It would seem, if the evolutionary hypothesis is true, that there would be ample evidence of the progression of certain lower forms all the way up the evolutionary ladder to the higher forms. The evidence for such *vertical progression* is not to be found. Dr. Gerritt Miller, who served on the staff of the Smithsonian Institution, writes the following:

> The complete absence of any intermediate forms between the major groups of animals, which is one of the most striking and most significant phenomena brought out by zoology, has hitherto been overlooked, or at least ignored.[7]

Dr. G. Ledyard Stebbins adds,

> . . . no transitional forms are known between any of the major phyla of animals or plants.[8]

Dr. George Gaylord Simpson has also written of this matter:

> In spite of these examples, it remains true, as every paleontologist knows, that *most* new species, genera, and families, and that nearly all new categories above the level of families appear in the record suddenly and are not led up to by known, gradual, completely continuous transitional sequences.[9]

---

6. "Analysis of So-called Evidences of Evolution," *Creation Research Society 1966 Annual*, III, No. 1 (May, 1966), 4.

7. Gedney, "Geology and the Bible," *Modern Science and Christian Faith*, ASA, p. 35, quoting Miller from A. H. Clark, *The New Evolution*, p. 189ff.

8. *Processes of Organic Evolution* (Englewood Cliffs, N.J.: Prentice-Hall, 1966), p. 144.

9. *The Major Features of Evolution* (New York: Columbia University Press, 1953), p. 360.

Dr. Edwin K. Gedney points out the sudden appearance of the various invertebrate forms:

> ... all the invertebrate phyla appear contemporaneously with marked suddenness in the Cambrian differentiated into phyla, classes, and orders, and with no clear indication as to how they developed into this condition if they did develop at all. [10]

Dr. J. D. Thomas also comments on the absence of transitional fossils:

> ... there are no transitional fossils or "missing links" between the phyla or larger groupings of animals. A *horizontal radiation* by which we mean "changes" *within* smaller groups, is accepted as true by conservative people. For example, we mean that all human beings—pygmies, giants, black or white, have come from an original pair, Adam and Eve. ... There are fertile hybrids, and "changes" between groupings not formerly recognized or accepted, but there are no links of any kind known between humans and animals, or between the major groupings of animals. ... In view of the true fact that so far as we know all life appeared suddenly, and of the fact that we definitely know that all life for which we have fossil evidence appeared suddenly, and that each of the basic phyla appeared suddenly, and no basic one of them has become extinct but all have continued through without change into the present, and further, that even many instances of what might be termed "lowly organisms" have continued on without any change, we actually have more data for believing in creation than anyone has for believing in evolution. This is further emphasized when we recognize that there has been "horizontal radiation," or change within groups, but no evidence of "vertical change," or "transition fossils" between major groupings. [11]

10. *Modern Science and Christian Faith*, p. 31.

11. "The Present Status of the Doctrine of Organic Evolution," in *Christian Faith in the Modern World: The Abilene Christian College Annual Bible Lectures* (Abilene, Texas: A.C.C. Students Exchange, 1960), pp. 165-166, 167.

GEOLOGICAL TIME SCALE*

AZOIC		4 to 5 billion years ago
ARCHAEOZOIC	Obscure	
PROTEROZOIC		
PALEOZOIC		540 million years ago
Cambrian	Trialobites	
Ordovician	Fish	
Silurian	Reptiles	
Devonian	Amphibians	
Mississippian	Insects	
Pennsylvanian		
Permian		
MESOZOIC		200 million years ago
Triassic	Dinosaurs	
Jurassic	Mammals	
Cretacious	Birds	
CENOZOIC		60 million years ago
Paleocene	Modern Mammals	
Eocene		
Oligocene		
Miocene		
Pliocene		
Pleistocene		
Recent	Man	2 million years ago

*Note: This is the standard, theoretical geological time scale in general use by
paleontologists and is to be found in most school textbooks on science.

The tentative or hypothetical nature of the commonly used "Geological Time Scale" is implied by the methods through which this system was devised. For example, William Smith, who lived from 1769 to 1839 and who is often called the "father of English geology" is credited with having "formulated the principle that strata must be placed in space and time according to the fossils that they contain."[12] The question then arises as to how scientists can know the age of the fossils so that they can date the rocks by the age of the fossils. The answer is given, "We know the age of fossils by the kind of rock or sediment in which they are found." It appears that basically the method has been to date the rocks by the fossils, and to date the fossils by the rocks. R. H. Rastall, Lecturer on Geology at Cambridge University ad-

12. *Book of Popular Science*, Vol. I, p. 314.

mitted this circular reasoning, in his article in the *Encyclopedia Brittanica.*[13]

Summary

Admittedly, changes have occurred and do occur in both plant and animal life. However, the evidence seems to indicate that these changes are of relatively limited extent. While they are more widespread than the modern term "species," they still are within the various families or groups. To put it another way, while there has been extensive change, this change seems to demonstrate the idea of *horizontal radiation,* rather than that of *vertical progression.* This appears to be reasonable in view of the almost complete absence of intermediate forms between the phyla or larger groupings of animals and plants. Dr. Walter Edward Lammerts gave this summary of the situation: ". . . the variations we see in the animate world . . . clearly point to a remarkably wise Creator who made living creatures capable of a limited amount of variation, so as to be able to survive even in the ever changing conditions of a world more adverse than that in which they originally were created."[14] That there has been change all admit. The question is whether the change is sufficient to establish the theory of a progression from the simplest forms of life on up the evolutionary ladder to the most intricate forms of life. The evidence supporting this view of universal, upward progress seems to be very incomplete, to say the least.

---

13. "Geology," *Encyclopedia Brittanica,* X (1936), 168.
14. "Things a Fruit Rancher's Boy Learned," *Evidence of God in an Expanding Universe,* p. 118.

18

Suggested Evidences of Evolution

It is generally true in our day that evolutionists assume the truthfulness of the evolutionary hypothesis in most of the textbooks and other books which they write. Perhaps the absence of evidence for the theory in the usual textbook results from the widespread acceptance of the theory by the general public. The writers feel no need to try to prove that the theory is true, since it is so widely accepted. However,the thoughtful student wants to know what evidence there is to support the theory. It is legitimate to ask for such evidence concerning a matter which has such far-reaching influence.

The evidence suggested by proponents of the evolutionary theory falls into five major categories: (1) the fossil records of living things, (2) comparative anatomy, (3) embryology, (4) vestigial organs, and (5) new characteristics. While there is some evidence in each of these areas to suggest the possibility of the evolutionary theory, there are also serious problems and questions in each area. Let us look at each area and evaluate its evidential support for this theory.

(1) Fossils

Dr. Austin H. Clark, a scientist for many years connected with the Smithsonian Institution in Washington, writes:

> No matter how far back we go in the fossil records of previous animal life upon the earth we find no trace of any animal forms which are intermediate between the various major groups of phyla. . . . The greatest groups of

animal life do not merge into one another. They are and
have been fixed from the beginning. . . . No animals are
known even from the earliest rocks which cannot at once
be assigned to their proper phylum or major group. . . .
There can be only one interpretation of this entire lack of
any intermediates between the major groups of animals. . . . If we are willing to accept the facts at their face
value we must believe that there were never such intermediates, or, in other words, that these major groups
from the very first bore the same relation to each other
that they do at the present day.[1]

On another occasion Dr. Clark further discussed the inadequacy of the fossil record:

So we see that the fossil record, the actual history of the
animal life on the earth, bears us out in the assumption
that at its very first appearance animal life in its broader
features was in essentially the same form as that in which
we now know it. . . . Thus so far as concerns the major
groups of animals, the creationists seem to have the
better of the argument. There is not the slightest evidence
that any one of the major groups arose from any other.[2]

Dr. John W. Klotz mentions the sudden appearance of the
various groups of animals:

In what is known as the Cambrian period there is literally
a sudden outburst of living things of great variety. Very
few of the groups which we know today were not in
existence at the time of the Cambrian period. One of the
problems of this Cambrian outburst is the sudden appearance of all of these forms. All of the animal phyla are
represented already in the Cambrian period except two
minor soft-bodied phyla (which may have been present
without leaving fossil evidence) and the chordates. Even
the chordates may have been present, since an object
which looks like a fish scale has been discovered in
Cambrian rock. It is hardly conceivable that all these

---

1. *The New Evolution, Zoogenesis* (Baltimore: Williams and Wilkins, 1930), pp. 129ff.
2. "Animal Evolution," *The Quarterly Review of Biology* (December, 1928), p. 539.

forms should have originated in this period. And yet there is no evidence for the existence of many of them prior to the Cambrian period.[3]

Dr. George Gaylord Simpson also says of the sudden appearance of fossils in the Cambrian era that "the change is great and abrupt. This is not only the most puzzling feature of the whole fossil record but also its greatest apparent inadequacy."[4] Later, Simpson says, "It is a feature of the known fossil record that most taxa appear abruptly. They are not, as a rule, led up to by a sequence of almost imperceptibly changing fore-runners such as Darwin believed should be usual in evolution."[5]

Dr. Klotz comments upon the absence of transitional forms in the history of animal life on the earth:

> Another problem is the absence of what are generally known as missing links—transitional forms—to show the development of the different phyla, classes, orders, etc. In mammals the earliest and most primitive known members of every order already have the basic ordinal characters. This is true of almost all orders of all classes of animals, both vertebrate and invertebrate. It is also true of the classes and of the phyla of the animal kingdom, and presumably it is also true of the plants. Simpson points out that the absence of these transitional fossils is a serious problem which cannot easily be dismissed. He says that in the larger groups—classes, orders and phyla—transitional groups are not only rare, but practically absent.[6]

Simpson points out the lack of progress toward a goal in the fossil records:

> The fossil record shows very clearly that there is no central line leading steadily, in a goal-directed way, from a protozoan to man. . . . Moreover, we do not find that

---

3. *Genes, Genesis, and Evolution,* p. 208.
4. "The History of Life," in *Evolution After Darwin,* Vol. I, *The Evolution of Life,* ed. Sol Tax (Chicago: University of Chicago Press, 1960), p. 144.
5. Simpson, p. 149.
6. Klotz, p. 215.

life has simply expanded, branching into increasing diversity, until the organisms now living had evolved. On the contrary, the vast majority of earlier forms of life have become extinct without issue.[7]

Oswald Spengler, commenting upon the absence of transitional fossils and the stability of fossil forms, put the matter in very strong terms:

> There is no more conclusive refutation of Darwinianism than that furnished by paleontology. Simple probability indicates that fossil hoards can only be test samples. Each sample, then, should represent a different stage of evolution, and there ought to be merely "transitional" types, no definition and no species. Instead of this we find perfectly stable and unaltered forms persevering through long ages, forms that have not developed themselves on the fitness principle, but *appear suddenly and at once in their definitive shape;* that do not thereafter evolve towards better adaptation, but become rarer and finally disappear, while quite different forms crop up again. What unfolds itself, in ever-increasing richness of form, is the great classes and kinds of living beings which *exist aboriginally and exist still, without transition types,* in the grouping of today.[8]

Cordelia Erdman Barber gives this evaluation of the fossil record:

> Fossils do not prove evolution. Neither do they disprove it. They strongly suggest that a considerable amount of descent with modification has transpired. They also exhibit a lack of transitional forms which may or may not be significant of limits of relationship.[9]

Limitations in the fossil record are pointed out by Dr. Everett C. Olson:

7. "The Nonprevalence of Humanoids," *Science* (February 21, 1964), p. 773.

8. *The Decline of the West,* trans. Charles Francis Atkinson, Vol. II (New York: Alfred A. Knopf, 1929), p. 32.

9. "Fossils and Their Occurrence," *Evolution and Christian Thought Today,* ed. Mixter, p. 151.

We are unable to make observations through lengths of time that even remotely approach those apparently necessary to accomplish the sorts of changes seen in the fossil record. Modern theory projects its generalizations from observations of very small changes over short periods of time, both in kind and in quantity, to account for all evolutionary change.[10]

Dr. G. Ledyard Stebbins draws the following conclusion:

The bias inherent in the fossil record is exactly of the wrong kind for evolutionists who wish to learn how the major groups of organisms originated.[11]

As a kind of summary we might point out that the fossil record neither proves that evolution has taken place nor does it disprove it. In an area where the evolutionist needs to find substantial verification for his theory, the evidence is inadequate. It is so incomplete that to base an elaborate theory upon it seems unwarranted.

(2) Comparative Anatomy

A second area used to support the theory of evolution is that of comparative anatomy—the idea that various animals are very much alike in both their skeletal structure and in certain vital organs. It is argued that these similarities indicate that the more advanced organisms are simply later, more refined models of the earlier organisms. Among the primates, for example, since the kidney of the chimpanzee is so similar to the kidney of man, there have been instances of kidney transplants. While these have not been very successful, the argument still has a convincing ring to many people. If there is such similarity, this view holds, there might well be implied a common origin.

---

10. "Morphology, Paleontology, and Evolution," *Evolution After Darwin*, Vol. I, *The Evolution of Life*, ed. Sol Tax, p. 533.

11. *Processes of Organic Evolution*, pp. 134-135.

Dr. Klotz points out certain problems and questions in the comparative anatomy position:

> Evolutionists also believe that similarities in structure and form indicate development from a common ancestor. The fact that the wing of a bat is more like the arm of a man than like the wing of a bird indicates to them that the bat and man are more closely related by descent than the bat and the bird. However, the fact that there are such things as parallel mutations again casts serious doubt on the correctness of this conclusion. Moreover, it is known that similarities are not always produced by the same genes. Nor can these resemblances be traced back to early embryonic development. There are also similarities which are ignored because they do not fit with evolutionary theories. Then, too, these relationships also vary at different stages in the organisms' development.[12]

Dr. Klotz next examines certain aspects of the chemical make-up of the various animals:

> Evolutionists place much stress today on the evidence from comparative physiology and biochemistry. Here similarities in chemical make-up and in functioning are stressed. Blood has been studied in this connection in considerable detail. Yet the relationships are not always those which they should be. Moreover, there are some relationships which are ignored. Then, too, the very complexity of chemical structure and of functioning casts serious doubt on the idea that such complexities could develop by chance.[13]

Dr. Klotz argues finally the reasonableness of the creationist's point of view in connection with the evidences of comparative anatomy:

> It is but natural that organisms which are supposed to occupy the same place in the scheme of life should have similar characteristics. There is no reason at all why God should have to follow a separate pattern in the creation

---

12. Klotz, p. 178.
13. Klotz, pp. 178-179.

of each organism. Indeed, Goethe and Oken, early sys-
tematists, regarded the existence of structural plans common to a large number of animals as evidence of some
form of planning in the act of creation. To them it
pointed to God as the Creator. They believed that classification showed the existence of a limited number of
archetypal ideas in the mind of the Creator, and they did
not regard it as being inconsistent with special creation.[14]

While it is true that certain parts of man's body are similar
to certain parts in the bodies of primates, this does not prove
that man is a descendant of these primates. It is just as logical
to believe that the Creator God made both. General Motors
cars all have some similarity of appearance and some similarity of parts, not because they descend from one another, but
because they originated in the minds of the same automotive
designers. The similarities among the various living things, in
the same way, may well be demonstrating that they originated in the mind of the same master architect rather than
that they descended one from the other.

(3) Embryology

The argument is sometimes made by evolutionists that the
human embryo goes through the various stages that its ancestors are alleged to have gone through in their evolutionary
development. The stages through which an infant goes during
the nine months of normal pregnancy are supposed to give
evidence of evolution because there are certain generalized
similarities in the stages through which the embryo passes.

The traditional statement of this point is found in the
textbook, *Introduction to Evolution,* by Paul Amos Moody:

"Ontogeny recapitulates phylogeny." [Haeckel, 1905].
Ontogeny is the life history of the individual, starting
with the ovum; phylogeny, as the term was used by

---

14. Klotz, p. 128, with brief quotation from Julian Huxley, *Evolution: The
Modern Synthesis* (New York: Harper & Brothers, 1942), p. 391.

Haeckel, is the series of adult ancestors of the individual in question. Haeckel maintained that in some way the adult condition of an ancestor is pushed back into embryonic development so that embryos of descendants pass through that ancestral adult stage. We shall see presently, for example, that in one stage the human embryo resembles a fish embryo.[15]

Dr. Klotz evaluates this view:

Embryology is also supposed to bring evidence in favor of the evolutionary theory. Much is made of resemblances during embryonic life, both general resemblances and specific resemblances. Yet a careful study of these indicates that many of these are superficial. At times the development is along lines of increasing complexity to meet the needs of the developing organism. Many of the structures do not have the function of comparable structures in other organisms. There are also embryonic resemblances which are deceptive. Today the recapitulation theory has been replaced by a number of other theories, such as paedomorphosis, neoteny, and fetalization. These theories, too, are open to a number of objections.[16]

(4) Vestigial Organs

The argument concerning vestigial organs as an evidence to support the evolutionary theory is explained and also evaluated by Dr. Klotz:

It is believed that the existence of so-called "vestigial organs" is another evidence of change that has taken place in the course of evolutionary development. Essentially this is a Lamarckian argument, for it depends on the idea of a degeneration through disuse. It should be pointed out that these supposedly functionless organs may have functions that have not yet been discovered. It is also possible that their functions are taken over by other organs when they are removed. We are by no means certain that the appendix, for instance, is a functionless, vestigial organ. Moreover, there are some vestigial organs

---

15. Moody, pp. 50-51.
16. Klotz, p. 179.

which prove too much. They indicate functions which no one believes the organ ever had.[17]

The history of the study of vestigial organs is one in which there is an ever-decreasing number of such organs. If one examines the textbooks of a few generations back, he finds a long list of organs that were listed in this category. Today, however, the list is very much shorter and is growing shorter year by year, as medical science is discovering the functions and purposes behind many of the organs that were formerly listed as carryovers from the past. To base an elaborate theory of evolution, to any significant degree, upon this area seems highly questionable.

(5) New Characteristics

The theory of evolution requires that down through the ages there has been the development of new characteristics in the various species of animals and vegetation. At first, it was thought that Lamarck's explanation was a valid explanation of these changes. Dr. Klotz also assesses this view:

> The fourth postulate is the most important of Lamarck's postulates, and, like the second, it is no longer accepted in scientific circles today. This principle is usually called the inheritance of acquired characteristics. It was disproved by Weismann, a champion of Darwinism, who cut off the tails of twenty-two generations of mice and found that the tails of their descendants were no shorter than those of a similar group whose tails had not been cut off.[18]

Concerning the phenomenon of blind fish, which have been found in certain caves Dr. Klotz writes the following:

> The blind fish to be found in caves in various parts of the world, for instance, are often stated to have originated in keeping with the use and disuse theory of Lamarck. It is

---

17. Klotz, p. 178.
18. Klotz, p. 25.

believed that seeing fish wandered into the subterranean streams and in the course of living there for centuries lost their vision because it was not used or needed. Packard, one of the outstanding students of this habitat, believes that their development cannot be explained on the basis of natural selection alone but that Lamarckianism in a modern form is necessary to explain their development.[19]

Of the type of characteristics which can be passed on from a parent to its offspring, Dr. Klotz gives this evaluation, one generally accepted by science today:

> So far as the fourth postulate is concerned, biologists today would say that the correctness of this statement depends upon whether the character is a somatic or germinal character. A somatic character is one which is determined by the environment rather than by the genes and chromosomes, the tiny structures within the cell which determine heredity. Such a character would be the powerful biceps developed by a blacksmith. Somatic characters are not inherited. Germinal characters are those characters which are determined by the genes and chromosomes, and these characters are inherited.[20]

Next, Dr. Klotz points out that the upward, progressive hypothesis inherent in the evolutionary theory has often been contradicted in nature:

> Darwin's theory requires that the differences between species have survival value. It follows from this requirement that the course of evolution will be ever upward, that there will be constant improvement within the species and among the different species. Accordingly, only those characteristics which are useful and helpful should develop in the organism in the course of evolution. Characteristics which are of no adaptive significance or are actually harmful to the organism should be quickly eliminated from the species.
> Now, as a matter of fact, in the course of evolutionary

---

19. Klotz, pp. 26-27, citing A. S. Packard, "The Cave Fauna of North America," *Memoirs of the National Academy of Science*, IV, (pt. 1), 116-143.
20. Klotz, p. 34.

history as outlined by the evolutionists themselves, there have been a great many nonuseful characteristics—characteristics which are either useless or else actually harmful to the organism. For instance, there are the dorsal spines of the Permian reptiles . . . which apparently elongated to such a degree that they proved to be harmful to these animals and brought about their extinction. Similarly extinction seems to have come to the saber-toothed "tiger," . . . as a result of the gradual lengthening of the canine or eye teeth. Another animal that appears to have become extinct because of harmful developments in the course of its history is the Irish Deer. . . . The antlers of this animal became so . . . heavy that they apparently brought about its extinction.[21]

The development of new or different characteristics, within relatively limited bounds, is admitted by all who have carefully observed life on the earth. The creationist believes that this is simply an evidence of the divine Creator's genius in creating life so that it can adapt to its environment and thereby survive. The evolutionist, on the other hand, believes that this phenomenon is an evidence of the natural development of life as it climbs the evolutionary ladder. The evidence given above would seem to indicate that the creationist has at least as good a position in this area of evidence as the evolutionist, and probably the better of the two positions, since the development of new characteristics stays within rather limited bounds and since these new characteristics have often been harmful and sometimes fatal.

Summary

When the conscientious student examines the areas in which supporting evidence for the theory of evolution is thought to be found, he comes away somewhat surprised and perhaps even a bit disappointed. The fossil record of life is far from complete and also falls far short of demonstrating the

---

21. Klotz, pp. 39-40, citing Simpson, *Tempo and Mode in Evolution* (New York: Columbia University Press, 1944), p. 171.

upward progress of animal and plant life claimed by the evolutionist. The similarities of bodily form and of certain organs among various animals can be as well explained by their having a common Creator, as by their having had a common ancestry. If God created all life, it is not unreasonable to believe that there would be similarity in body-structure and body-function of certain animals and plants.

The argument from embryology is one of analogy, a type of argument that logicians generally agree is not useful as proof. Analogies make clear, but do not prove. While it may be true that the various stages in the development of a single plant or animal are in a rough general way like the theoretical stages of the entire evolutionary hypothesis, this does not constitute real proof. Vestigial organs, to an ever smaller degree, as modern scientific studies increasingly discover the uses of the glands and organs, can be offered as evidence supporting the evolutionary theory. On the matter of new characteristics, the creationist has at least as good a position as that of the evolutionist, when he claims that the development of new characteristics, always within a rather limited range, are merely evidence of God's endowing His creation with the ability to adapt to the environment. Since these new characteristics come from the latent possibilities within the genes, and since they are always within rather narrow limits, they hardly constitute evidence of the broad upward sweep which the theory of evolution requires. It is also noted that often these new characteristics are harmful rather than helpful, a fact which hardly fits the evolutionary hypothesis. All in all, the areas where the evolutionist needs to find extensive support for his theory have proved disappointing.

19

Possible Mechanisms of Evolution

Turning now from the areas of evidence where support for the evolutionary hypothesis is sought, we look at the mechanism for the theory. If evolution has occurred and is the basic explanation of all life, then surely there is some obvious system or mechanism for it. There must be some demonstrable means by which it operates. We now look at four possibilities.

(1) Natural Selection

From the very beginning, Charles Darwin suggested that the mechanism was natural selection and the survival of the fittest. Careful examination of this idea has revealed that it is less than adequate and has resulted in the search for other possible mechanisms. Robert Heath Lock points out the inadequacy of this view to explain how evolution could achieve what it claims:

> No one questions the validity of natural selection as a means of exterminating types which are unfitted for their environment—there is clearly a tendency for the fittest types to survive, once they have come into existence. . . . But, when this is admitted, it does not necessarily follow that natural selection . . . has been the method by which these adapted forms have originated.[1]

---

1. *Variation, Heredity, and Evolution* (London, 1920), p. 61, quoted by George McCready Price, *The Phantom of Organic Evolution* (New York: Fleming H. Revell, 1924), p. 193.

George McCready Price quotes Paul Kammerer of Vienna and Prof. E. W. MacBride of England who ask how natural selection is going to start a single organ of a single organic type. They then follow this question with the taunt that "if it cannot *start* anything, what is the use of invoking its supposed ability to improve the structures after they have all been built?"[2]

Natural selection has the ability to choose those characteristics which are within the capability of an animal or plant, as determined by the genes, but this theory does not have the capability of bringing new characteristics into existence. It is this latter requirement which the theory of evolution must have if it is to be proved true. The survival of the fittest can be demonstrated, but the arrival of the fittest is the problem.

(2) Mutations

A second mechanism by which the theory of evolution might have functioned is that of mutations. This is a more likely possibility since mutations do change the genes, the hereditary determiners of life. However, there are problems in this theory also, as Thomas D. S. Key notes:

> As biologists became more aware of laws of heredity, it became progressively more evident that species must do more than simply "improve" by a mere selection of the fit. It was discovered that in order to acquire new organs a species must acquire new genes (hereditary determiners inside each cell). How could this happen in the light of the hereditary law that "like begets like"? Hugo de Vries, the Dutch botanist . . . noted what appeared to be rare but striking exceptions to the "like begets like" law. . . . [He thought] that evolution occurs, not gradually as Darwin believed, but visibly and suddenly in great jumps. Many genuine examples of hereditary changes have since been found on the gene level, and are known variously as saltations, mutations, mutants, sports, and "freaks."

---

2. *The Phantom of Organic Evolution,* pp. 191-192.

... de Vries' mutationism (announced in 1901) ... never succeeded in becoming completely established. De Vries intended only to supplement natural selection, not to supplant it.

Although mutationists could rally such noteworthy examples as the Shetland pony, Kentucky wonder bean, change in eye color in the fruit fly ... and others, they were faced with a growing number of insistent problems such as the following: (1) the number of original mutations of all kinds is extremely low; (2) beneficial mutations are far less common than neutral, harmful, or fatal ones; and (3) mutations have never been observed to produce new organs.[3]

Dr. Robert E. D. Clark, of the faculty of Cambridge University in England, also discusses the problem:

In mutations, therefore, we have the only kind of heritable variation known to science upon which natural selection might work in order to produce new varieties and species. Yet, although many thousands of mutations have now been studied, not a single clear instance has been found in which a mutation has made an animal more complicated, brought any new structure into existence or even effected any new adaptation of a radical nature.[4]

Dr. John W. Klotz points out the negative characteristics of most mutations:

The chief difficulty in the way of evolution by mutation is the fact that most mutations are either lethal or semilethal. Either they kill the organism outright—in which case they are said to be lethal—or they are harmful in some way, so that in the ordinary course of events they would be eliminated. These latter are said to be semilethal mutations. They include mutations in which the fertility rate is reduced, mutations which result in the loss of certain organs, and the like. The Ancon mutation is an example of a semilethal mutation. Winchester says that

---

3. "The Influence of Darwin on Biology," *Evolution and Christian Thought Today*, ed. Mixter, pp. 25-26.

4. *Darwin: Before and After* (London: The Paternoster Press, 1948), p. 131.

over 99 percent of the mutations which have been studied in various forms of life are harmful in some degree.[5]

Frederick S. Hulse points out further problems with this mechanism:

> Mutations occur at random, not because it would be convenient to have one. Any chance alteration in the composition and properties of a highly complex operating system is not likely to improve its manner of operation and most mutations are disadvantageous for this reason. There is a delicate balance between an organism and its environment which a mutation can easily upset. One could as well expect that altering the position of the foot brake or the gas pedal at random would improve the operation of an automobile.[6]

Finally, Dr. Klotz gives this summary of the situation:

> In a summary we must say that mutations appear at first glance to supply a very promising mechanism for evolution. It does look very much as if this may be the mechanism for supplying the variety on which natural selection may work. A more careful analysis of this phenomenon, however, shows a great many problems and casts serious doubt on the idea that mutations supply the necessary mechanism for evolution. For one thing, most mutations are either lethal or semilethal. There is real doubt that any are really favorable. The chance, moreover, that a mutation will be preserved in the stock, even if favorable, is very slight. Mathematical calculations show this very clearly. Reverse mutations, which seem to occur rather frequently, would certainly slow down evolution. Moreover, there are many restrictions on mutations: restrictions on the direction of mutation, mutation suppressors which reduce the mutation rate, restrictions imposed by parthenogenesis, and the like.[7]

The improbability, or even impossibility, of evolution bringing about the conditions which we find in the world

5. *Genes, Genesis, and Evolution*, p. 282.
6. *The Human Species* (New York: Random House, 1963) p. 53.
7. Klotz, pp. 305-306.

today is sometimes admitted. Take, for example, a statement from Julian Huxley, one of the foremost exponents of evolution today:

> A proportion of favorable mutations of one in a thousand does not sound much, but is probably generous, since so many mutations are lethal, preventing the organism living at all, and the great majority of the rest throw the machinery slightly out of gear. And a total of a million mutational steps sounds a great deal, but is probably an underestimate—after all, that only means one step every two thousand years during biological time as a whole. However, let us take these figures as being reasonable estimates. With this proportion, but without any selection, we should clearly have to breed a thousand strains to get one with one favorable mutation; a million strains (a thousand squared) to get one containing two favorable mutations; and so on, up to a thousand to the millionth power to get one containing a million.
>
> Of course, this could not really happen, but it is a useful way of visualizing the fantastic odds against getting a number of favorable mutations in one strain through pure chance alone. *A thousand to the millionth power, when written out, becomes the figure 1 with three million noughts after it: and that would take three large volumes of about five hundred pages each, just to print!* [Italics supplied]. Actually, this is a meaninglessly large figure, but it shows what a degree of improbability natural selection has to surmount, and can circumvent. One with three million noughts after it is the measure of the unlikeliness of a horse—the odds against it happening at all. *No one would bet on anything so improbable happening; and yet it has happened.* [Italics supplied]. It has happened, thanks to the workings of natural selection and the properties of living substance which make natural selection inevitable.[8]

The use of mutations as the mechanism by means of which evolution takes place sounds so plausible at first, but ultimately seems so improbable. Surely there is some mechanism more promising than this.

---

8. Julian Huxley, *Evolution in Action*, a Mentor Book (New York: The New American Library, 1957), pp. 41-42.

(3) Uniformitarianism

The evolutionary hypothesis is based upon a faith in uniformitarianism. Concerning this whole assumption Dr. Morris writes the following:

> This faith may be in the doctrine of uniformity, which assumes that these present processes may be extrapolated indefinitely into the past or future and that therefore "all things continue as they were from the *beginning* of the Creation" (II Peter 3:4). If one, because of his basic presupposition, wishes to believe in uniformity in this way, it is logically possible for him to do so and to explain all the pertinent data in this context. He can determine the ages of rocks and suns by projecting present rates of change into the limitless past; he can develop theories about the evolution of species and life and galaxies and chemical elements and everything in the universe, if he wishes, and no one can prove him wrong, for the simple reason that these events are not reproducible and therefore not subject to scientific checking. The most that can be done is to argue that his theories are either probable or improbable on the premise of his own uniformitarian presupposition, depending upon the logical consistency of the superstructure he has erected upon this foundation. But this is all within the context of his pure assumption—his faith— of uniformity. One can equally logically start with some other assumption and then develop his explanations of the data within that framework.[9]

P. D. Krynine writes:

> Conventional uniformitarianism, or "gradualism," i.e., the doctrine of unchanging change, is verily contradicted by all post-Cambrian sedimentary data and the geotecnonic histories of which these sediments are the record. Thus, quantitative interpretations of the Ordovician from the Recent are meaningless.[10]

---

9. Morris, p. 109.
10. "Uniformitarianism Is a Dangerous Doctrine, "*Journal of Paleontology,* 30 (1956), 1004.

(4) Hybridization

This is simply the careful breeding of plants and animals in such a way as to select desirable characteristics and to eliminate undesirable ones. No really new characteristics are achieved. A better strain of corn is achieved, but it is still corn. This type of development of slightly different plants and animals is, of course, very common throughout the modern world. The whole system of breeding cattle, of developing better strains of various food-producing plants, and other such matters are within the realm of hybridization. There are very definite limits, however, as to what combinations can be achieved. Also, and this is the fundamental fact, all of this cross-breeding can only bring out the characteristics that are latent in the genes of the various animals and plants. Nothing fundamentally new is developed.

Summary

As we look at the various mechanisms which have been claimed as the means by which evolution has progressed through the centuries, we find more problems than we find answers. Natural selection will not account for what is claimed. Mutations, while promising at first, are disappointing to the evolutionist because they are generally negative and harmful. Uniformitarianism is an assumption itself and can hardly be the absolute proof that the evolutionary hypothesis requires. Hybridization is no proof at all. One wonders just how the evolutionary hypothesis has gained so wide a hold upon the modern world in view of the inadequacy of the support of the theory both in areas of evidence and in possible mechanisms by which it could have happened.

20

Theistic Evolution

The theistic evolutionist holds a position somewhat between that of the absolute evolutionist and the creationist. He believes that God created the materials of our universe and then guided and superintended the process by which all life has evolved from the very simplest one-celled form on up to the sophisticated forms which we know today. Evolution was God's method of bringing about the present development, though originally the materials were created by God.

Dr. Edward Luther Kessel presents the theistic evolution point of view:

> Once He had established the material of Nature, and the laws of Nature to govern its activities, He used this mechanism to continue creation—creation by evolution (evolvement, development). . . . Just as an open-minded scientist must heed the evidence and recognize that there must be a God, the non-scientist must likewise heed the evidence and recognize that creational evolution was God's method of creation, once He had produced the material of the universe and established its laws. . . . Natural selection is one of the chief mechanisms of evolution, just as evolution is a mechanism of creation. . . . The species produced through natural selection are just as much created by God as if they had been manufactured by Him. Natural selection in itself cannot create anything. . . . These variations, from which natural selection selects, result from mutations (changes) which are the products of the laws of genetics . . . and these do not

behave according to blind chance as the materialistic evolutionists would have us believe.[1]

Another author who presents the theistic evolution point of view is Paul Amos Moody:

It is just as possible to worship a God who works through natural laws, slowly evolving life on this planet, as it is to worship a God who creates by sudden command. In fact, is not our concept of the Creator immeasurably heightened when we understand more and more of the intricate workings of this marvelous universe? Such a Creator is of far greater stature than would be a miracle worker who created things once and for all back in 4004 B.C.[2]

Dr. J. D. Thomas evaluates the theistic evolutionist's position and presents a number of problems faced by this position:

The real problem in considering theistic evolution is whether atheistic or naturalistic, mechanical evolution has been proved. . . . The theory means that all known forms of life have developed into their present major classifications and minor classifications from one or two original cells or maybe even "naked genes." . . . What are the arguments against atheistic evolution, by way of summary?

1. The atheists have no evidence or information about the beginning of life on the earth. . . .

2. The suddenness of the appearance of fossil forms of life . . . well developed into major classifications or different phyla, which phyla still extend into the present time.

3. There are no transition fossils between the simpler and the more complex forms of life. . . .

4. There is no evidence whatever of change from one phylum into another or crossing-over between phyla. . . . Instead of a rare or occasional missing link, the whole chain is missing. . . .

5. There is no adequate theory of a mechanism to explain how evolution occurred. . . .

---

1. "Let's Look at Facts, Without Bent or Bias," *The Evidence of God in an Expanding Universe,* ed. Monsma, pp. 51-53.

2. *Introduction to Evolution,* p. 496.

6. The doctrine requires chance occurrence far beyond the range of reasonable probability. . . .

7. The doctrine of evolution allows for no purpose or directiveness in the universe. . . .

8. The evolutionists can not explain mind, spirit, values or conscience. . . .

9. Biological evolution has ended. This is an embarrassing thought to an evolutionist today, for if the greatest thing in the world is the "laws of nature," then why have they changed course? Why are new forms not continually evolving? Why cannot we look around us today and see all kinds of in-between forms that are on their way up to something higher and better?[3]

If evolution has not occurred, it then becomes unnecessary to deal with the question of theistic evolution. These unsolved problems suggest that evolution has not occurred.

Dr. G. A. Kerkut, Professor of biochemistry at the University of Southampton and one of the twentieth century's most outstanding British biologists, has recently pointed out some of the assumptions of evolution and some of the basic problems which this hypothesis faces:

May I here humbly state as part of my biological *credo* that I believe that the theory of Evolution as presented by orthodox evolutionists is in many ways a satisfying explanation of some of the evidence. At the same time I think that the attempt to explain all living forms in terms of an evolution *from a unique source,* though a brave and valid attempt, is one that is premature and not satisfactorily supported by present-day evidence. It may in fact be shown ultimately to be the correct explanation, but the supporting evidence remains to be discovered. We can, if we like, believe that such an evolutionary system has taken place, but I for one do not think that "it has been proven beyond all reasonable doubt."[4]

In his opening chapter Dr. Kerkut continues:

Before one can decide that the theory of Evolution is the best explanation of the present-day range of forms of

3. *Facts and Faith,* Vol. I, pp. 179-182.
4. *Implications of Evolution* (London: Pergamon Press, 1960), p. vii.

living material one should examine all the implications that such a theory may hold. . . . There are, however, seven basic assumptions that are often not mentioned during discussions of Evolution. Many evolutionists ignore the first six assumptions and only consider the seventh. These are as follows:

(1) The first assumption is that non-living things gave rise to living material, i.e., spontaneous generation occurred.

(2) The second assumption is that spontaneous generation occurred only once.

The other assumptions all follow from the second one.

(3) The third assumption is that viruses, bacteria, plants and animals are all interrelated.

(4) The fourth assumption is that the Protozoa gave rise to the Metazoa.

(5) The fifth assumption is that the various invertebrate phyla are interrelated.

(6) The sixth assumption is that the invertebrates gave rise to the vertebrates.

(7) The seventh assumption is that within the vertebrates the fish gave rise to the amphibia, the amphibia to the reptiles, and the reptiles to the birds and mammals. Sometimes this is expressed in other words, i.e. that the modern amphibia and reptiles had a common ancestral stock, and so on.[5]

These assumptions form the general theory of evolution and are by their nature not capable of experimental verification. Even though some of these processes may be simulated today, this shows only that such processes are possible; it does not prove that they have occurred.

In the Centennial Edition of Darwin's *Origin of Species,* we find an unexpected disclaimer concerning the theory of evolution. A challenging introduction by Professor W. R. Thompson, R.F.S, formerly Director of the Commonwealth Institute of Biological Control, Ottawa, Canada, completely reverses the adulatory verdict of Darwin and his work written by Sir Arthur Keith twenty-five years ago:

---

5. Kerkut, p. 6.

As we know, there is a great divergence of opinion among biologists, not only about the causes of evolution but even about the actual process. This divergence exists because the evidence is unsatisfactory and does not permit any certain conclusion. It is therefore right and proper to draw the attention of the non-scientific public to the disagreements about evolution. But some recent remarks of evolutionists show that they think this unreasonable. This situation, where scientific men rally to the defence of a doctrine they are unable to define scientifically, much less demonstrate with scientific rigour, attempting to maintain its credit with the public by the suppression of criticism and the elimination of difficulties, is abnormal and undesirable in science.[6]

It would be hard to find a more decisive rebuttal than this to the whole problem of evolution as an accepted scientific "fact."

Summary

What I have hoped to do in this area of study is to show that the doctrine of evolution today is really only an expression of a faith on the part of those who hold it. That there has been a great deal of change (*horizontal radiation*) no one denies; that this change has demonstrated the truth of the evolutionary hypothesis (*vertical progression*) has not been proved. Rather than teach evolution as a proven fact, it is my conviction that it should be presented only as an hypothesis or a theory.

From time to time I am asked the question, "What about the theistic evolutionist? Do you believe that he can be saved?" First of all, I must point out the obvious. I am not the judge. Only God knows who will be saved and who will be lost. It is both unbecoming and presumptuous for any human being to declare whom God will save. It is possible, of course, to refer to plain teachings within the Scriptures, where God's Word has declared that certain ones will be saved

---

6. "Introduction to Darwin's Theory," in Charles Darwin, *Origin of Species*, Everyman's Library (London: Dent, 1967), p. xxii.

and certain others will be lost. For example, man is not judging when he points out that faith is a requirement of those who would be saved, for the Scriptures plainly say, ". . . and without faith it is impossible to be well-pleasing unto him; for he that cometh to God must believe that he is, and that he is a rewarder of them that seek after him" (Heb. 11:6). Similarly, one is not passing his own judgment when he states that salvation is possible only in Christ for again the Scriptures are explicit on this subject: "Jesus saith unto him, I am the way, and the truth, and the life: no one cometh unto the Father, but by me" (John 14:6). In the absence of a statement about what God will do with one who has *misunderstood* the manner in which He brought the world into existence and produced life on the earth, it is impossible for us to speak dogmatically.

The problem has sometimes been presented to me in this fashion. "Here is a man who believes in the existence of God, the divinity of Christ, the inspiration of the Scriptures, and the importance of the church. He has become a Christian in the manner prescribed in the New Testament, and he faithfully worships and works according to the directions in the Scriptures; yet he believes that God created the universe and then developed life on the earth by the evolutionary method. He is a faithful Christian and at the same time a theistic evolutionist. Will he be lost because of this view?" To say that such a man would be lost because of his misunderstanding and mistaken ideas about how God produced life on earth would be to speak where one has no real right to speak.

Would one be lost for believing that Isaac was the father of Abraham, rather than the other way round? Would one be lost for believing that Jacob had only ten sons instead of twelve? Would one be lost if he felt that the flood was only a localized phenomenon, covering only a few hundred square miles, rather than the whole earth? Would one be lost for thinking that Bishop Ussher's dates are correct, when they now appear to be somewhat incorrect? In other words, will God determine salvation in terms of what one believes about how or when he created the universe? Will one be lost because of a misunderstanding or a misinterpretation of Genesis 1? It is my conviction that we ought to be slow to speak on these matters.

From the foregoing pages, it ought to be clear to anyone that I am not an evolutionist, theistic or otherwise. I have not yet seen sufficient evidence to lead me to believe in the evolutionary theory. At the same time, I am not ready to exclude from fellowship sincere Christian brethren who mistakenly (as I believe) think that evolution was God's method. To allow this particular issue to divide the Lord's church would be most unfortunate indeed. It certainly would be most pleasing to Satan, and most displeasing to God.

Afterword

Before bringing this chapter to a close I feel obligated to register what I feel about the distressingly negative effects which the general acceptance of the theory of evolution has had and continues to have upon our modern world. Some of the most obvious trends of our day are: (1) The trend toward materialism with less and less concern for spiritual matters, (2) the trend away from the moral principles taught in the Bible and toward a greater and greater degree of permissiveness, (3) the trend toward more and more crime, until crime is presently rising ten times faster than the population is growing, according to J. Edgar Hoover, Chief of the F.B.I., (4) the trend away from respect for all forms of authority, including that of parents, teachers, church leaders, and leaders of government, (5) the trend toward less and less self-discipline, and (6) the trend toward atheism and the loss of religious faith. It is my conviction that the widespread teaching and general acceptance of the evolutionary hypothesis is responsible in a major way for these trends. If a person comes to believe that he is only a graduate beast, that there is no God behind our existence, that there is no judgment to come, and that there is no eternal life hereafter, why should he not live as he pleases?

Along these same lines, the words of Dr. A. E. Wilder Smith are appropriate:

> A hundred years ago Professor Adam Sedgwick of Cambridge remarked, after reading and digesting the *Origin of Species* by Darwin, that if this book were to find general public acceptance, it would bring with it a brutalization of the human race such as it had never seen before. Dr. R. E. D. Clark remarks that in our generation we have seen the fulfillment to the hilt of Sedgwick's prophecy. Hitler and Mussolini glorified struggle and war on the basis that the fittest would survive and the race would be thus cleansed. Stalin used any force at his disposal to trick his enemies or rob banks to supply money for "the party." Like the Fascists and National Socialists, his power policy was one of "no holds barred."[7]

Above everything else, modern man needs to return to his faith in the existence of a loving heavenly Father who created all things, including man himself. He needs to remember that he is created in the image of God and that he will be responsible for his life at a final great day of judgment, after which he will, if he is a faithful Christian, spend eternity with God.

My own personal convictions on this whole issue of evolution grow out of a high estimate of man. The Bible teaches us that man is created in the image of God—that he is essentially different from every other creature. Man's dignity is proclaimed not just in the creation story of Genesis, but throughout the entire Bible. The apostle Paul put it, "We are also his offspring" (Acts 17:28). This conception of man is the basis of all human rights—the "inalienable rights" of our Constitution. An ox has no such rights. We can kill a hundred fine steers in Chicago and no one says a word, but let a hundred people be killed in an aircrash and the nation is disturbed. Human life is sacred. Our forefathers freed the

---

7. *Man's Origin, Man's Destiny: A Critical Survey of the Principles of Evolution and Christianity* (Wheaton, Ill.: Harold Shaw, Publishers, 1968), pp. 190-191. (He refers to R.E.D. Clark, *Darwin, Before and After* [Chicago: Moody Press, 1967]).

slaves a century ago because of these peculiar human rights. In our Western civilization everything we believe in is based upon the view that man is an immortal being. I reject as false philosophy anything that debases man. Man has not come without plan or purpose out of nothing. In the deepest sense the theory of evolution is not true.

Part Four

The Inspiration of the Bible

> . . . .*in the Christian view of things it is the self-contained God who is the final point of reference while in the case of the modern view it is the would-be self-contained man who is the final point of reference* . . . .
>
> —*Cornelius Van Til*

21

What Does Inspiration Mean?

There are several different ideas concerning the inspiration of the Bible. Perhaps it would be more accurate to say that different men believe in different levels of inspiration. Some of the more common ideas are the following:

1. *Universal inspiration.* This is the idea that certain men of genius are inspired in the sense that they are exceptionally talented. In this sense Shakespeare was inspired; Michaelangelo was inspired; Beethoven was inspired. However, this is not really inspiration at all, but merely exceptional talent. It might be called genius, but not inspiration.

2. *Partial inspiration.* This view holds that the Bible is inspired in its great principles and ideals, but not in its historic facts, statements of doctrine, and minute rules and regulations. This theory of inspiration takes the authority of God away from the Scriptures, leaving men to determine what is good and what is not. It, too, is an unacceptable theory of inspiration.

3. *Plenary or full inspiration.* This view holds that men wrote exactly what God wanted them to write, without errors or mistakes, yet with their own personalities in evidence. This is sometimes called verbal inspiration. It holds that the original autographs of the Scriptures were inspired and fully authoritative, for they came as the Holy Spirit guided men to write. This is the conviction which we hold.

We hold to plenary, or verbal inspiration of the Bible because it is taught clearly in the Scriptures themselves. For example, the apostle Peter wrote, ". . . . no prophecy of scripture is of private interpretation. For no prophecy ever came by the will of man: but men spake from God, being moved by the Holy Spirit" (II Pet. 1:20-21). Making the matter even clearer was a statement from the apostle Paul: "But we received, not the spirit of the world, but the spirit which is from God; that we might know the things that were freely given to us of God. Which things also we speak, not in words which man's wisdom teacheth, but which the Spirit teacheth; combining spiritual things with spiritual words" (I Cor. 2:12-13).

We do not contend that the Holy Spirit dictated the Scriptures to the men who wrote them, but that the Holy Spirit guided and superintended their writing so that it was exactly what God wished said and in a manner fully in keeping with the facts and with His will. It is obvious that the different styles indicate different writers and a certain amount of freedom in writing. The same is true of the different vocabularies used by the various writers. For this reason we do not hold the dictation view of the Scriptures, but rather that the Scriptures were "spirit breathed" or "inspired" of God. Dr. Benjamin B. Warfield wrote, "Inspiration is, therefore, usually defined as a supernatural influence exerted on the sacred writers by the Spirit of God, by virtue of which their writings are given Divine trustworthiness."[1]

Areas of Supporting Evidence

There are six major areas in which meaningful evidence is found supporting the idea that the Scriptures are the inspired Word of God. These areas of support, in the order in which they are presented in this book, are as follows:

1. The Scriptures claim to be inspired.
2. The influence of the Bible is an evidence that it is from God.

---

1. *The Inspiration and Authority of the Bible* (Philadelphia, Penn.: Presbyterian and Reformed Publishing Co., 1948), p. 131.

3. The unusual style of the Scriptures suggests inspiration.

4. The unity of the Scriptures is evidence of inspiration.

5. The fulfilled prophecies of the Scriptures indicate inspiration.

6. The scientific foreknowledge of the Bible suggests inspiration.

We now turn to an examination of some of the evidence under each of these headings.

The Scriptures Claim Inspiration

There is "an air of infallibility" about the writings that make up the Bible. The writers of the Scriptures were often unlearned and ignorant men—fishermen, farmers, tax-collectors, and the like. Yet, these men wrote with supreme confidence that they were speaking God's message. Several thousand times, in one way or another, the men who wrote the Scriptures claim to be speaking from God. This is impressive due to the fact that there is no self-consciousness about their claims. Had they been ordinary men, writing on their own, they would have felt some need to bolster their claims with expressions such as, "Now, it may be difficult for you to believe this, but I am speaking from God. . . ." We find no such tell-tale give-a-ways in their writings. They announce unequivocally that they are revealing God's message with no embarrassment or recognition that this is in any way unusual.

The direct claims of inspiration on the part of the writers of the Scriptures are also very impressive in view of their limited backgrounds. For the most part these men had little formal education and were in no position to do the exalted writing that we find them doing. Neither from the standpoint of the manner in which they wrote, nor from the standpoint of the message which they presented can we explain the finished product in terms of who they were and the backgrounds of training which they had. How could such men have come to know such great truths, and how could they have come to make such great claims of speaking for God, if

God had not truly told them what to write? Dr. Henry Thiessen states it well:

> How could uninspired man write a book that commands all duty, forbids all sin, including the sin of hypocrisy and lying, denounces all human merit as insufficient for salvation, holds out as man's only hope faith in the atoning death, physical resurrection, and present intercession of Christ, and condemns to hell for all eternity all who reject this one way of salvation and persist in sin?[2]

Influence of the Bible

There is a universally accepted principle, "Water never rises higher than its source." The Bible itself states the same principle, "By their fruits ye shall know them" (Matt. 7:16). James also mentions this same general principle in asking, "Doth the fountain send forth from the same opening sweet water and bitter? can a fig tree, my brethren, yield olives, or a vine figs? neither can salt water yield sweet" (James 3:11-12). The point is this. Wherever the Bible has gone civilization has been lifted to a higher plane. It has made better husbands and wives, better fathers and mothers, better sons and daughters, and better employers and employees. It has been the strongest influence for good in the history of the world. Could this influence for good have come from a source which was itself a fabrication and a collection of false claims? Knowing what we know about cause and effect, we cannot but conclude that the good influence of the Bible is another evidence that it within itself is eminently good.

Many of the major institutions of our modern world were created by the teaching and influence of the Scriptures. Many of the laws that make our land a pleasant place in which to live also came from the teaching of the Bible. Without its beneficent influence, our world would be an infinitely worse place in which to live.

---

2. *Introduction to the New Testament* (Grand Rapids, Mich.: Wm. B. Eerdmans Publishing Co., 1950), p. 85.

Henry Rogers wrote a book, *The Eclipse of Faith,* in which he imagined that some powerful hand had wiped the influence of Christ out of civilization, as a hand might wipe the chalk writing from a chalkboard in a schoolroom. He dreamed that he went into his library and found many of his law books with blank paragraphs, that he went into his picture gallery and found many of his finest pictures with blank canvases in their frames, and that he examined many of the great anthologies of poetry only to find blank pages where some of the world's finest poetry had been before. He dreamed that in driving downtown he found great gaping holes where buildings had vanished. There had been on these locations such institutions as schools, hospitals, orphanages, old peoples' homes and the like. But now, with the influence of Christ removed from the world, all were gone. Then, this lawyer cried out, "I would not want to live at all in a world where Christ were not." We think that Henry Rogers had a very forceful way of conveying an idea which is absolutely true. We would borrow his idea and say that the same can be said for the Bible. Without its great influence for good, our world would be a tragic place in which to live.

Summary

The evidence for the inspiration of the Scriptures includes evidence from the men who did the writing. These were not highly educated men, yet they gave to the world the finest statements of morals and ethics that the world has ever known. Their manner of writing was also exceptionally fine. Even with all of our additional education and training, men today do not write so well. Surely this is an evidence that these men were guided by God. There is also the fact that these men claimed to be speaking from God, with no sense of embarrassment or self-consciousness. They believed that they were delivering God's message.

Further, the influence of the Scriptures is of such a nature that it can indicate only that the source from which this influence came was good. If the Bible had been a great hoax or deception, it could not have had the influence toward the uplifting of civilization that it has had. These are two of the reasons that I believe the Bible to be a book uniquely given by God.

22

The Unusual Style of the Scriptures

A study of word style is not particularly inspiring to most students. While there are many who have done well in the study of grammar and composition, the very nature of this field is not such as to be especially stimulating. Yet, in the style in which the Bible is written there is a very impressive evidence that the writers were guided by the Holy Spirit of God. There are five areas in which the style of the Scriptures is impressive:

1. The brevity of entire books.
2. The brevity of Bible incidents.
3. The omissions of the Scriptures.
4. The impartiality of the Scriptures.
5. The calmness of the Scriptures.

We shall examine each of these areas in which the style of the Scriptures shows unusual characteristics which suggest the superintendence of God.

The Brevity of Entire Books

The Book of Genesis has only fifty chapters, yet it tells of the origin of the world and all that is in it. The first twenty-five hundred years of man's history on the earth is covered in these same chapters. The first thirty-four verses tell of the creation of the material universe, the plant world, the animal world, and man. This contrasts sharply with the volubility of the newspapers and magazines of our day. The average sports reporter takes more space to tell about a high school basketball game than Moses was guided to take in telling about the creation of the universe. *Readers' Digest* each month uses more words than God's book used to tell about the first twenty-five hundred years of man's history on earth. Later, in telling the story of Christ, Matthew used only twenty-eight chapters, Mark used only sixteen, Luke used only twenty-four, and John used only twenty-one. If the writers of these and other books of the Bible had been writing with the same freedom that men use ordinarily, their accounts would have been many times as long as we find them in the Scriptures.

The Brevity of Bible Incidents

Genesis 3:1-24 tells the story of man's fall. In this small space we have the explanation of the origin of sin, suffering, sickness, death, toil, and the necessity of the coming of a Messiah. The baptism of Jesus is described in Matthew 3:13-17. This important story is told in only five verses, or seventeen half-lines in an ordinary Bible. Mark and Luke use only nine half-lines to tell of this significant event. The transfiguration of Jesus is described in Matthew 17:1-8. This event is told in eight verses, or twenty-five half-lines, yet the account tells of Moses and Elijah coming back from the dead and also declares the very important message of the superiority of Christianity over the old law.

Christ's appearances after his death and resurrection were among the most significant events mentioned in the New Testament. However, Matthew tells of only two of these appearances, Mark tells of only three, Luke tells of only three and John tells of only four. Altogether there were at least ten of these appearances to His disciples immediately after His resurrection. The persecutions administered by Saul of Tarsus and his spectacular conversion are mentioned in Acts 9:1-2, 20-21. This unusually important event is described casually and briefly, though it must have been of great significance in the early church. The death the apostle James is mentioned briefly in Acts 12:2. "And he killed James the brother of John with the sword." Actually only eleven words are used to tell of the death of the first apostle martyr. One wonders why. There are many questions that normally would have been answered. How did he face death? What was the reaction of the disciples? Where and how was he buried? Yet, none of these answers are given in the brief account of this first significant martyrdom of an apostle. Again, men on their own, do not write with such restraint.

The Omissions of the Scriptures

John's Gospel omits the account of the birth of John the Baptist, and of Jesus' birth, genealogy, youth, baptism, temptation, transfiguration and ascension. Neither Mark nor John mentions anything in the first thirty years of Christ's life. There is no virgin birth, no genealogy and no childhood in their accounts. In contrast, an ancient work of the second century, called the *Protoevangelium,* devotes twenty-five chapters to the supposed events between the annunciation to Mary and Herod's slaughter of the innocents. Another ancient work, *The Gospel of the Infancy,* devotes fifty chapters to the first twelve years of Christ's life. Neither of these books is inspired, and their contents are highly imaginary, but they do show the normal tendency in the writings of men.

The apostle John told of only twenty different days of the Lord's life and ministry. The total life of Christ covered more than 12,000 days, and His active ministry more than 1,270 days, yet all of the Gospel narratives together tell of events which happened on only some 34 different days in the life of Christ. Out of the 879 verses in the Gospel of John, 237 pertain to one day of Jesus' life. Writing under this God-given restraint, it is no wonder that John said, "Many other signs therefore did Jesus in the presence of the disciples, which are not written in this book: but these are written, that ye may believe that Jesus is the Christ, the Son of God; and that believing ye may have life in his name" (John 20:30-31). He also said, "And there are also many other things which Jesus did, the which if they should be written every one, I suppose that even the world itself would not contain the books that should be written" (John 21:25). This figure of speech, hyperbole, is an indication of John's own desire to tell very much more concerning his Lord.

The Book of Acts tells of the events in the lives of only Peter and Paul, omitting the events connected with the lives of the other apostles. The Book of Acts does not tell of the trial of Paul before Nero, though this was a matter of great interest when the book was written and through all succeeding history. The apostle Paul condensed several volumes of events into a single list, as indicated in II Corinthians 11:24-27, where he said, "Of the Jews five times received I forty stripes save one. Thrice was I beaten with rods, once was I stoned, thrice I suffered shipwreck, a night and a day have I been in the deep; in journeyings often, in perils of rivers, in perils of robbers, in perils from my countrymen, in perils from the Gentiles, in perils in the city, in perils in the wilderness, in perils in the sea, in perils among false brethren; in labor and travail, in watchings often, in hunger and thirst, in fastings often, in cold and nakedness." How much more he would like to have said! Obviously there was a restraint upon the writers of the Scriptures.

Finally, most impressive of all, there is no physical description of Jesus in the Bible. Even though the men who wrote about Him loved Him with an intensity that has been unsurpassed in the annals of history and even though they confidently believed that He was the divine Son of God, for some reason they did not describe how He looked. There is no indication of His height, the color of His eyes, the color of His hair, nor any aspect of His physical make-up. We might well remember that some of the world's finest sculpturing had already been done when Christ lived upon the earth, just a few miles away in Greece. Had it been God's will, not only could the likeness of Jesus have been clearly conveyed in the words of the writers of His biography, but also in the imperishable stone which has preserved the likeness of so many ancient men of prominence and influence. Obviously, it was God's will that no physical description or physical likeness of Jesus be handed on to future generations.

The Impartiality of the Scriptures

The writers of the Bible set forth both the virtues and follies of those of whom they wrote. The lives of both friends and foes were described in a direct, factual manner, rather than in the style found in most literature, where friends are praised and enemies are vilified. As examples, note the account of the lives of Abraham and Sarah, as we read of them in Genesis 12:10-20 and Genesis 20:1-12. In these passages serious flaws are mentioned in the life of Abraham, even though he was the exalted father of the Hebrew race. Similarly, David, generally considered Israel's greatest king, is pictured in a very embarrassing light, as the story of his adultery, deception, and murder in connection with Bathsheba, the wife of Uriah, is told in II Samuel 11:1-21.

In the New Testament we read of the ugly anger of the apostles James and John in connection with a Samaritan village, as told in Luke 9:51-55. We also read of the ambition of the mother of James and John, when she came to Jesus to ask preferment for her sons, as told in Matthew 20:20-28. There is also the embarrassing story of Peter's denial of Christ, as told in Matthew 26:69-75. The betrayal of Jesus by his disciple Judas is also fully described in Matthew 26:14-16, 47-50.

The impartiality of the Holy Spirit is obvious. There are no apologies for Peter, no reproaches for Judas, just the facts. Had men been writing in the ordinary manner they would undoubtedly have ignored some of the flaws, especially of the leaders of God's people, or at the least they would have tried to explain away some of these obvious faults. We are grateful that in the Scriptures the facts are given just as they happened.

The Calmness of the Scriptures

The wonderful and the commonplace are described alike in the Bible. The emotions of the writers are never apparent, even though they must have been deeply involved emotionally in what they were writing about. As an example, the climactic transfiguration of Jesus is described in Matthrew 17:1-5, in these very ordinary words, "And after six days Jesus taketh with him Peter, and James, and John his brother, and bringeth them up into a high mountain apart: and he was transfigured before them; and his face did shine as the sun, and his garments became white as the light. And behold, there appeared unto them Moses and Elijah talking with him. And Peter answered, and said unto Jesus, Lord, it is good for us to be here: if thou wilt, I will make here three tabernacles; one for thee, and one for Moses, and one for Elijah. While he was yet speaking, behold, a bright cloud overshadowed them: and behold, a voice out of the cloud, saying, This is my beloved Son, in whom I am well pleased; hear ye him." Similarly, there is a calmness in the description of the murder of John the Baptist, as told in Matthew 14:6-12.

Christ's miracles such as the feeding of the five thousand, as told in Mark 6:39-44, His walking on the water, as told in Mark 6:49-51, and His raising of Lazarus from the dead, as told in John 11:43-46, are described in very simple, commonplace terms. There is none of the emotional excitement that must have been present. Even the events of Gethsemane on the night of Christ's betrayal are told without anger or invective, in Matthew 26:14-16, 47-56.

The crucifixion, central event in Christ's ministry, is described without emotion in Matthew 27:33-56. Likewise the resurrection, as pictured in John 20:11-20, is without the colorful adjectives that men would normally have used. In the same way, the remarkable beginning of the church on Pentecost, with three thousand being baptized that first day, as described in Acts 2:40-42, is mentioned without the colorful description that men would normally have given such an event. One asks, "Where are the human adjectives: *amazing, unbelievable, unprecedented, stupendous, colossal, unrivaled?*" They are not there. The writers of the Bible, in the very style in which they wrote, indicate that they were being guided by the Holy Spirit.

Summary

The significance of all of these facts is apparent. Men do not write like this. The only possible explanation for the brevity of the Scriptures, the omissions of the Scriptures, the impartiality of the Scriptures, and the calmness of the Scriptures is that God guided and limited the writing. Remember, too, that many of these were unlearned and ignorant men—fishermen, tax-collectors, and the like. Truly the Bible is God's book. We must study it to learn God's will for us. We must obey its commands in order to please God and be saved.

23

Unity, Prophecies, Scientific Foreknowledge

The Unity of the Scriptures

The sixty-six books of the Bible were written by approximately forty different men, over a period of nearly sixteen hundred years. The first books of the Old Testament were written by Moses, about 1500 B.C., and the last book of the Bible was written by the apostle John, approximately A.D. 100. The writers of the Scriptures used different languages and lived in different countries, yet they presented one central theme, without variation or contradiction. They used two languages primarily, Hebrew and Greek, with small portions in Aramaic. In many instances the writers had no access to the other books of the Bible dealing with events of their own time, yet they wrote in perfect unity, each complementing that which the others had written.

This unity of the Scriptures could not have been achieved except that God guided the various writers. John William Haley, in his book, *Alleged Discrepancies of the Bible,* deals with 975 so-called discrepancies in a rather satisfying way. Many of these problems are very ancient. They cover the entire field of alleged discrepancies. James Orr, speaking of the Moslem, Zoroastrian, and Buddhist scriptures, said:

> It is the simple fact that there is nothing that can be properly called history in these other sacred books of the world. They are, as every student of them knows, for the most part jumbles of heterogeneous material, loosely

placed together, without order, continuity, or unity of
any kind. There is no order, progress, or real connection
of parts. . . . The Bible, on the other hand, is a history
with a beginning, a middle, and an end; a history of
revelation; the history of a developing purpose of God,
working up to a goal in the full-orbed discovery of the
will of God for man's salvation in His Son Jesus Christ.
There is nothing like this, nothing even approaching it, in
any other collection of sacred books in the world.[1]

Unguided, men could not have achieved this great degree of
unity.

Fulfilled Prophecies

Before pointing out some of the prophecies in the Scriptures it is well to deal with the question, "What is prophecy?" The word prophecy involves two complementary
meanings: forth-telling and fore-telling. The primary meaning
at the time the Old Testament Scriptures were written was
probably in the realm of forth-telling, meaning the proclaim-
ing or preaching of God's message, though the element of
fore-telling was also present and became more meaningful
with the passing of time.

Prophecy deals with events and human affairs which do
not happen in a causal order, but are unpredictable. A prophecy must be more than a good guess. It must possess sufficient
accuracy as to be capable of verification. Predictions in
science deal with causal order and are not prophetic predictions. C. P. M'Ilvaine, in his book, *The Evidences of Christianity,* defined prophecy as, "a declaration of future events,
such as no human wisdom or forecast is sufficient to make;
depending on a knowledge of the innumerable contingencies
of human affairs, which belongs exclusively to the omniscience of God; so that, from its very nature, prophecy must
be divine revelation."[2] The argument from prophecy is essen-

---

1. *The Bible Under Trial* (New York: A. C. Armstrong, 1907), pp. 287-288.
2. *The Evidences of Christianity,* 7th ed. (New York: Harper & Brothers, 1847), p. 185.

...at from omniscience, since limited human ...future only if it is told them by an omni- ...s, in predictive prophecy, God informs the ...ture.

...tain characteristics of Bible prophecy that ...dered. Real prophecy is peculiar to the Bible. ...rophecy is not an incidental, or accidental, ...means of establishing the creditability of the ...religions claim some prophetic elements, but none pla.... strong emphasis upon prophecy that the Old Testament does. Deuteronomy 18:9-22 and Isaiah 41:22-23 indicate this special usefulness of prophecy.

In many cases the prophecy found in the Scriptures is very minute in its specifications. Prophecy frequently dealt with the very remote in time and with people or kingdoms that did not as yet exist. An example is found in Daniel 2. The fulfillment of prophecy was clear, not equivocal or ambiguous. One real case of fulfilled prophecy would establish a supernatural act. Prophecy is occasionally of a nature as to be in exact opposition to what unguided human intelligence would predict. This was especially true of the prophecies concerning great cities or civilizations whose doom was predicted. Examples would include the cities of Jerusalem, Nineveh, and Babylon.

In order to reduce the effective power of prophecy, liberals and critics of the Bible have charged: (1) that the language is oftentimes vague, (2) that some of the prophecies are artificially fulfilled, (3) that some of the prophecies were written after the events, and (4) that the same phenomenon occurs in other religions. On this last point we quote Randolph S. Foster's words from his *Evidences of Christianity, the Supernatural Book:*

> No well accredited prophecy is found in any other book or even oral tradition now extant, or that has ever been extant in the world. The oracles of heathenism are not to be classed as an exception. There is not a single one of

them that meets the tests required to prove supernatural agency, which every scripture prophecy evinces.[3]

C. P. M'Ilvaine adds the following:

The history of pagan nations, indeed, abounds with stories of auguries, and oracles, and detached predictions. . . . But what an immeasurable distance separates all the pretended oracles of paganism from the dignity of the prophecies in the Bible. The avowed end of the former was to satisfy some trivial curiosity, or aid the designs of some military or political leader. . . . Who could think of comparing such pitiful mockeries of divine omniscience with the dignified, and sublime, and holy prophecies which are spread out so openly and widely in the scriptures?[4]

Specific Predictions and Their Fulfillments

In order that the reader may study at his own leisure, the following list of prophecies is submitted, with suggestions concerning the meaning of the prophecy and its fulfillment. This material is quoted in abbreviated form, and adapted, from Bernard Ramm:

1. **Hosea**
   a. Hosea 1:4, 5, 7. These verses stated that Israel, as a military force and as a national commonwealth, was to pass out of existence. Just the opposite is predicted of Judah. The opposite predictions of the histories of Israel and Judah, and their remarkable fulfillment imply the divine guidance of Hosea.
   b. Hosea 3:4. Here is an amazing prediction that Israel shall be without a king or prince; shall be without a priestly ministry; and shall be without idolatry. This latter point especially could hardly have been guessed by human wisdom.
2. **Joel**
   a. Joel 2:28-32. This passage contained a promise with the following items:

3. (New York: Hunt & Eaton, 1889), p. 111.
4. M'Ilvaine, pp. 191-192.

1. That the Spirit of Jehovah would be poured out in an unprecedented measure;
2. That all flesh would be recipients of it;
3. That unusual manifestations would accompany it (dreams, visions, and prophecies);
4. That there would be no differentiations of sex;
5. That accompanied with it would be a gracious call to salvation;
6. That the call would extend to whomever God wished to extend it; and
7. That this was to be before a great and notable catastrophe would fall upon the Jewish people.

This entire prophecy was fulfilled in detail on Pentecost as described in Acts 2.

   b. Joel 3:4-8. This prophecy predicted that Tyre and Sidon would be destroyed as they had formerly destroyed certain portions of Judah. This occurred when Alexander the Great marched down the coast of Palestine.

3. Amos

   a. Amos 1:3-5. This prophecy predicted that the military strength of Damascus would be broken. It was fulfilled by Tiglath-pileser.

   b. Amos 1:6-8. This prophecy declared that Gaza, Ashdod, and Ashkelon would be destroyed. Hezekiah, Sennacherib, and Alexander the Great carried out the prophecy.

4. Obadiah

   a. This book contained the prophecy that the Edomites would be destroyed both by (a) the heathen and by (b) the Jews. Both came to pass.

5. Micah

   a. Micah 1:6; 3:12. These passages prophesied the destruction of Samaria and Jerusalem.

   b. Micah 5:2. This prophecy spoke of Bethlehem Ephratah and how that from it there would be that which would go out to bless the thousands. Obviously, this was a foretelling that Jesus would be born there. Matt. 2:6; John 7:42.

   c. Micah 4:10. This prophesied that God's people would be delivered into the hands of the Babylonians.

6. Nahum

This was a prediction and description of the destruction of Nineveh. It had a number of interesting details.

7. Zechariah

a. Zechariah 1:12-21. This passage suggested that the fortunes of Judah and Jerusalem were going to be better than those of previous generations. Zechariah 1:16: "My house shall be built."

b. Zechariah 2:10-11: "Sing and rejoice, O daughter of Zion: for, lo, I come, and I will dwell in the midst of thee, saith the Lord. And many nations shall be joined to the Lord in that day" (KJV). This seemed to be pointing to the time when the Son of God would be dwelling among the people and when His church should be established.

c. Zechariah 6:9-15. This was obviously a messianic prophecy of the coming of the Lord, the Branch.

d. Zechariah 9:9. This was likewise a clear-cut messianic prophecy: "Rejoice greatly, O daughter of Zion; shout, O daughter of Jerusalem: behold, thy King cometh unto thee: he is just, and having salvation; lowly, and riding upon an ass, and upon a colt the foal of an ass" (KJV). This passage was quoted in Matthew 21:4, 5 as fulfilled in the triumphal entry story.

e. Zechariah 11:12. This passage mentioned that the price of the Jews for the Messiah was thirty pieces of silver. It was quoted as being fulfilled in Matthew 26:14-15.

f. Zechariah 12:10. "And I will pour upon the house of David, and upon the inhabitants of Jerusalem, the spirit of grace and of supplications: and they shall look upon me whom they have pierced" (KJV). This was quoted twice by John (John 19:37 and Rev. 1:7) as fulfilled in the crucifixion.

8. Malachi

a. Malachi 1:11. "For from the rising of the sun even unto the going down of the same my name shall be great among the Gentiles; and in every place incense shall be offered unto my name, and a pure offering: for my name shall be great among the heathen, saith the Lord of hosts" (KJV).

b. Malachi 4:5. "Behold, I will send you Elijah the prophet before the coming of the great and dreadful day of the Lord: and he shall turn the heart of the fathers to the children, and the heart of the children to their fathers, lest I come and smite the earth with a curse" (KJV). This is quoted in Matthew 11:14 and Mark 9:11, 12 as fulfilled in John the Baptist.[5]

The following is a list of twenty-five Old Testament prophecies concerning Christ, along with the passages in the New Testament which show their fulfillment:

Prophecy	Fulfillment
1. Of the tribe of Judah (Gen. 49:10).	Luke 3:23-38.
2. Of the royal line of David (Jer. 23:5).	Matt. 1:1.
3. Born of a virgin (Isa. 7:14).	Matt. 1:18-23.
4. Born in Bethlehem (Micah 5:2).	Matt. 2:1-6.
5. A forerunner shall prepare the way (Mal. 3:1; 4:5).	Matt. 3:1-2; 11:7-14.
6. He shall enter Jerusalem riding upon an ass (Zech. 9:9).	Matt. 21:6, 7.
7. He shall be betrayed by a disciple (Ps. 41:9).	John 13:18.
8. Betrayal price stated (Zech. 11:12).	Matt. 26:14, 15.
9. Betrayal money to be returned (Zech. 11:13).	Matt. 27:3-7.
10. His disciples shall forsake him (Zech. 13:7).	Matt. 26:31, 56.
11. False witnesses shall accuse him (Ps. 35:11; 27:12).	Matt. 26:59-61.
12. He shall suffer abuse (Isa. 50:6).	Matt. 26:67.
13. He shall suffer in silence (Isa. 53:7).	Matt. 27:12-14.
14. He shall be stripped (Isa. 53:5).	Matt. 27:28, 29.
15. Hands and feet pierced (Ps. 22:16).	Luke 23:33; John 20:24-28.
16. Numbered with criminals (Isa. 53:12).	Mark 15:27.

---

5. *Protestant Christian Evidences* (Chicago: Moody Press, 1957), pp. 97-122.

17. To divide garments (Ps. 22:18).   John 19:23, 24.

18. Gall and vinegar to be offered (Ps. 69:21).   John 19:28, 29; Matt. 27:34.

19. No bones to be broken (Ps. 34:20).   John 19:33-36.

20. He shall be pierced (Zech. 12:10).   John 19:33-37.

21. The crowds shall rebuke him (Ps. 22:6-8).   Matt. 27:39-44.

22. Darkness in daytime to signal crucifixion (Amos 8:9).   Matt. 27:45.

23. To be buried with the rich (Isa. 53:9).   Matt. 27:57-60.

24. To arise from the dead (Ps. 16:10).   Matt. 28:6; Acts 2: 22-32; 13:32-37.

25. To ascend (Ps. 68:18).   Luke 24:51; Acts 1:9; Eph. 4:8-10.

Still another impressive list of prophecies concerning Christ was published in D. R. Dungan's *Hermeneutics* [Roman numerals changed to Arabic] :

1. He was to be the seed of the woman (Gen. 3:15; 4:2; Matt. 1:18).

2. He would be the Son of God (Ps. 2:7; Luke 1:32-35).

3. He would overcome the serpent (Gen. 3:15; Heb. 2:14).

4. The seed of Abraham (Gen. 12:1-3; 17:7; 22:18; Gal. 3:16).

5. The seed of Isaac (Gen. 21:12; Heb. 11:18).

6. The seed of Judah (Gen. 49:10; Heb. 7:14).

7. The seed of David (Ps. 132:11; Jer. 23:5; Acts 13:23; Rom. 1:3).

8. The time of His coming and death (Dan. 9:24-27; Luke 2:1).

9. Born of a virgin (Isa. 7:14; Matt. 1:18; Luke 2:7).

10. He was called Immanuel (Isa. 7:14; Matt. 1:22, 23).

11. Born in Bethlehem of Judea (Mic. 5:2; Matt. 2:1; Luke 2:4-6).

12. Great men shall come and bow down to Him (Ps. 72:10-15; Matt. 2:1-11).
13. Children slaughtered, that He might be killed (Jer. 31:15; Matt. 2:16-18).
14. Introduced by John the Baptist (Isa. 40:3; Mal. 3:1; Matt. 3:1-3; Luke 1:17).
15. Was anointed by the Holy Spirit (Ps. 45:7; Isa. 11:2; 61:1; Matt. 3:16, 17; John 3:34; Acts 10:38).
16. He was a prophet like unto Moses (Deut. 18:15-18; Acts 3:20-22).
17. He was sent as a deliverer to the people (Isa. 61:1-3; Luke 4:16-21, 43).
18. He is the light to Zebulun and Naphtali (Isa. 9:1-3; Matt. 4:12-16).
19. He comes to the temple and cleanses it (Hag. 2:7-9; Mal. 3:1; Luke 19:45; John 2:13-16).
20. His poverty (Isa. 53:2; Mark 6:3; Luke 9:58).
21. He was meek, and without ostentation (Isa. 42:1-2; Phil. 2:7-9).
22. His compassion (Isa. 40:11; 42:3; Matt. 12:15-20; Heb. 4:15).
23. Was without guile (Isa. 53:9; I Pet. 2:22).
24. Great zeal for the house of God (Ps. 69:9; John 2:17).
25. He taught by the use of parables (Ps. 78:2; Matt. 13:34-35).
26. He wrought miracles (Isa. 35:5, 6; Luke 7:18-23).
27. Rejected by His brethren (Ps. 69:8; Isa. 53:3; John 1:11; 7:5).
28. Hated by the Jews (Ps. 69:4; Isa. 49:7; John 15:24-25).
29. Rejected by their rulers (Ps. 118:22; John 7:48; Matt. 21:42).
30. A stone of stumbling and rock of offense (Isa. 8:14; Rom. 9:32; I Pet. 2:8).
31. Betrayed by a friend (Ps. 41:9; 55:12-14; John 13:18-21).
32. Forsaken by His disciples (Zech. 13:7; Matt. 26:31-56).
33. Was sold for thirty pieces of silver (Zech. 11:12; Matt. 26:15).
34. This money was given to buy the potter's field (Zech. 11:13; Matt. 27:7).

35. He was patient and silent in all His sufferings (Isa. 53:7; Matt. 26:63; 27:12-14).
36. Smitten on the cheek (Mic. 5:1; Matt. 27:30).
37. His sufferings were intense (Ps. 22:14-15; Luke 22:42-44).
38. Was scourged and spit upon (Ps. 35:15; Isa 50:6; Mark 14:65; John 19:1).
39. His visage was greatly marred (Isa. 52:14; 53:3; John 19:1-5).
40. He suffered that He might bear away our sins (Isa. 53:4-6; Dan. 9:26; Matt. 20:28; 26:28).
41. The rulers, Jews and Gentiles, combine against Him to put Him to death (Ps. 2:1-4; Luke 23:12; Acts 4:27-28).
42. He was extended upon the cross, and His hands and His feet were nailed to the wood (Isa. 25:10, 11; Ps. 22:16; John 19:18; 20:25).
43. This agony was increased by being numbered among thieves (Isa. 53:12; Mark 15:28 [sic. 27]).
44. They gave him gall and vinegar (Ps. 69:21; Matt. 27:34).
45. He was cruelly mocked (Ps. 22:7-8; 35:15-21; Matt. 27:39-44).
46. He suffered alone; even the Father's presence was withdrawn (Isa. 63:1-3; Ps. 22:1; Matt. 27:46).
47. They parted His garments among them, and cast lots for His vesture (Ps. 22:18; Matt. 27:35).
48. He thus became a curse for us, and bore our reproach (Ps. 22:6; 79:7; 9:20; Rom. 15:3; Heb. 13:13; Gal. 3:13).
49. He made intercession for the murderers (Isa. 53:12; Luke 23:34).
50. After His death they pierced Him (Zech. 12:10; John 19:34-37).
51. But did not break a bone of His body (Ex. 12:46; Ps. 34:20; John 19:33-36).
52. He was buried with the rich (Isa. 53:9; Matt. 27:57-60).
53. His flesh did not see corruption (Ps. 16:8-10; Acts 2:31).
54. He rose from death the third day, according to the Scriptures (Ps. 16:8-10; 30:3; Luke 24:6, 31, 34).
55. He ascended into the heavens (Ps. 68:18; 24:7-9; Luke 24:51; Acts 1:9).

56. He became a priest after the order of Melchizedek, who was king and priest at the same time (Ps. 110:4; Heb. 5:5-6; Zech 6:12-13).
57. He received for Himself a kingdom that embraces the whole world (Ps. 2:6; Luke 1:32; Dan. 2:44; 7:13, 14; John 18:33-37; Matt. 28:18, 19; Phil. 2:9-10).
58. His law went forth from Zion and His word from Jerusalem (Isa. 2:1-3; Mic. 4:12; Luke 24:46-49; Acts 2:1-40).
59. The Gentiles should be admitted into His service (Isa. 11:10; 42:1; Ps. 2:8; John 10:16; Acts 10:44-48; Rom. 15:9-12).
60. The righteousness of His reign (Isa. 9:6, 7; Ps. 45:6, 7; John 5:30; Rev. 19:11).[6]

Mathematics and Prophecy

What are the chance possibilities of making the foregoing statements concerning Christ hundreds of years before His birth and having these detailed statements verified by subsequent history? Dr. Hawley O. Taylor provides the answer:

Regarding these n cases of events foretold for Israel's Messiah who was to come, if the chances of success were even in the case of each one, that is p (probability) equals $\frac{1}{2}$ in every case, then the overall probability that all n events would find their fulfillment in one Person would be p^n equals $(\frac{1}{2})^n$. Thus there would be but one chance in 2^n (33 million, where n equals 25) of all these foretold events coming true if they were mere guesses. Now a glance at these prophecies concerning Christ reveals that they do not all have an even chance of success, for in some instances it is highly improbable that the event could occur at all (as for a child to be born without a human father). A very conservative compromise would be p equals $1/5$; and the overall probability for the n prophecies coming true would be p^n equals $(1/5)^n$, or one chance out of a thousand trillion if n equals 25.[7]

---

6. 3rd ed. (Cincinnati, O.: The Standard Publishing Co., n.d.), pp. 395-399.
7. Source unknown.

Even if the prophecy regarding the virgin birth be excluded, the number remains astronomically large, too large to assume that this accidentally happened!

Scientific Foreknowledge

Another of the evidences that the Bible is inspired is to be found in the area of scientific foreknowledge. *Negatively,* this argument holds that the Bible shows that something beyond man must have guided the writers of the various books, because we do not find the superstitions and wrong notions concerning scientific matters which were current in ancient times incorporated into the Scriptures. How easy it would have been for Moses to have slipped at one point or another, by including such things as the then believed hypotheses that the earth was flat and rested upon the back of some great turtle or some great elephant. The most natural thing would have been for the various writers to have included many superstitions which later would have been proved false. The absence of these is an impressive evidence that God must have guided and superintended the writers.

On the positive side, we find scattered evidences of advanced scientific understanding in the pages of the Bible. In the Book of Job, for example, we find the statement, "He stretched out the north over empty space, and hangeth the earth upon nothing" (Job 26:7). This indicated an advanced knowledge that was not common in the day when Job wrote. Similarly, in Isaiah 40:22, we find, "it is he that sitteth above the circle of the earth." This obviously indicated some idea of the roundness of the earth, an idea not to be discovered by men for many centuries. In Leviticus 13:45, there is this reading, "And the leper . . . shall cover his upper lip, and shall cry, Unclean, unclean . . . " This obviously was a recognition of the necessity of isolation in connection with certain diseases. This was not known by men generally for many centuries, though it is a common practice in our day, since we understand how diseases are communicated by germs.

Leviticus 14 gave another example in its commands that certain washing be done in running water. The command was given originally to the Israelites when they were wandering in the wilderness of Sinai, where water was very scarce. The necessity of washing in running water implied a knowledge of disease germs, which was not to be discovered by men for several thousand years.

We also find in the Scriptures accurate references to such matters as altitude. Whenever the Scriptures use the expression "going up," or the expression "going down," to a certain city we can be sure that they are accurate. Even though these references were given in a day when there were no scientific devices for measuring altitude, in some manner these references were correctly given in each case. If this is compared with the common man's ignorance of such matters in our own day, it will be all the more impressive. Most of us do not know whether it is up or down to any neighboring town about us. Even in these small details the Bible has an impressive accuracy and concern for details.

Summary

Certain characteristics of the Scriptures can hardly be explained except by the superintendence of the writing by the Holy Spirit. How could the remarkable unity of the Scriptures have been achieved if there were no one central mind guiding all the writers? How could the various prophecies of the Old Testament have been made hundreds of years before their fulfillment if there were no divine foreknowledge of future events? How could the writers of the Scriptures have anticipated certain scientific information and knowledge which was not to be discovered by men for many centuries? These are just additional areas that give us a confidence that the Bible is no mere book written by men. When one adds all of these evidences together, he is overwhelmed with the evidence that this book has a supernatural flavor to it. It must be, as it claims, a divine book given by God through men to men.

Part Five

Miracles

. . . in all these miracles alike the incarnate God does suddenly and locally something that God has done or will do in general. Each miracle writes for us in small letters something that God has already written, or will write, in letters almost too large to be noticed, across the whole canvas of Nature . . . they do close and small and, as it were, in focus what God at other times does so large that men do not attend to it. —C. S. Lewis

24

What Are Miracles?

In any thorough examination of the field of Christian Evidences it is necessary to include the consideration of supernatural events, or miracles. The word miracle is used in a number of different senses, which fact makes it necessary for us to define it at the very outset of this phase of our study. For example, *Webster's New Collegiate Dictionary* defines a miracle as "an event or effect in the physical world deviating from the known laws of nature, or transcending our knowledge of these laws; a wonder or wonderful thing; a marvel."[1] This definition is in keeping with the average man's use of the word in normal conversation. He speaks of man's landing on the moon and safe return to earth as a miracle. This, however, is not at all the definition which we wish to use in this chapter. There is nothing supernatural about this definition in which the word *miracle* is used to refer to anything that is not understood, or is especially complicated, or is just newly discovered.

On the other hand, C. S. Lewis defined a miracle as "an interference with Nature by supernatural power."[2] Even though short and incomplete, this is an accurate definition of the kind of miracles that one finds described in the Bible. *The Westminster Dictionary of the Bible* gives an even better definition: "Miracles are events in the external world, wrought by the immediate power of God and intended as a

---

1. (Springfield, Mass.: G. & C. Merriam Co., Publishers, 1949), p. 536.
2. From *Miracles* by C. S. Lewis. (New York: The Macmillan Company, 1947), p. 15. Used with permission.

sign or attestation. They are possible because God sustains, controls, and guides all things, and is personal and omnipotent."[3] This definition suggests that supernatural power (God) occasionally steps into our universe, setting aside normal, observable laws of nature, and does something beyond the ordinary. This, we believe, is what the Bible means when it speaks of miracles.

The Scriptures use a number of different words in referring to miraculous events. The American Standard Version of the Gospel according to John uses the word *signs* to refer to the seven occasions when a miraculous act is described. This is a good choice of terms, for, in the case of New Testament miracles especially, they were signs pointing toward something—usually the divinity of Christ or some related aspect of the Gospel. Occasionally these additional words are used in the Scriptures to refer to miracles: *tokens, wonders, powers,* and *mighty works.* Each of these is well chosen to suggest this supernatural activity on the part of God or one of His representatives. It is not thought that there is any special distinction intended between or among these several different words. All of them refer to what is generally known as a miracle, in the Biblical sense.

Revealed Word of God

The Bible is, we believe, the revealed Word of God. As indicated in previous chapters, the writers were moved by the Holy Spirit of God in their writing. When these men were writing about something concerning which they had human knowledge, their writings were superintended and guarded from error by the Holy Spirit. When they were writing about things which they could not know through their own observations and experiences, the Holy Spirit revealed the message to them. In all of their writings they were delivering God's intended message. The Bible, then, is a book which comes down from God, through men, to men. This is the

---

3. (Philadelphia: The Westminster Press, 1944), p. 399.

traditional, orthodox view and contains the idea of God working miracles. God, to put the matter another way, makes Himself known in history.

The following miracles, selected at random from both Old and New Testaments, do not provide a complete list of all the miracles in the Bible, though they do constitute a representative list of all Biblical miracles:

1. Creation (Gen. 1).
2. Flood (Gen. 6-8).
3. Confusion of tongues (Gen. 11:1-9).
4. Passage through the Red Sea (Exod. 14:22).
5. Manna (Exod. 16:4-31).
6. Quails (Exod. 16:13).
7. Aaron's rod buds (Num. 17:1-9).
8. Destruction of Nadab and Abihu (Lev. 10:1-2).
9. Balaam's ass speaks (Num. 22:23-30).
10. Sun and moon stand still (Josh. 10:12-14).
11. Destruction of Uzzah (II Sam. 6:1-8).
12. Elijah increases widow's meal and oil (I Kings 17:9-16).
13. Elijah raises the Shunamite's child (II Kings 4:18-37).
14. Hezekiah's cure (Isa. 38:21).
15. Jonah in the fish's belly, (Jon. 1:17; 2:10).
16. Deliverance of Shadrach, Meshach, and Abednego (Dan. 3:23-27).
17. Destruction of Sennacherib's army (II Kings 19:35).
18. Pillar of cloud and fire (Exod. 13:21-22; 14:19-20).
19. Transformation of Moses' face (Exod. 34:29-35).
20. Samson's strength (Judg. 14:5-6).
21. The incarnation of Jesus (Matt. 1:18-25).
22. The appearance of the star of Bethlehem (Matt. 2:2-10).
23. The deliverance of Jesus (Matt. 2:13-23).
24. Jesus turns water into wine (John 2:1-11).
25. Jesus heals the nobleman's son (John 4:46-54).
26. Jesus heals Peter's mother-in-law (Matt. 8:14-17).
27. Jesus heals the impotent man (John 5:1-16).
28. Jesus restores the centurion's servant (Matt. 8:5-13).
29. Jesus raises the widow's son to life (Luke 7:11-16).
30. Jesus stills the tempest (Mark 4:35-41).
31. Jesus casts devils out of two men of Gadara (Luke 8:26-39).

32. Jesus raises from the dead the daughter of Jairus (Mark 5:22-24, 35-42).
33. Jesus cures woman with the issue of blood (Matt. 9:20-22).
34. Jesus feeds five thousand people (John 6:5-14).
35. Jesus walks on the sea (Mark 6:45-52).
36. Jesus feeds four thousand people (Matt. 15:32-39).
37. Jesus restores one deaf and dumb (Mark 7:31-37).
38. Jesus restores a blind man (Mark 8:22-26).
39. Jesus restores ten lepers (Luke 17:11-19).
40. Jesus raises Lazarus from the dead (John 11:1-46).
41. Jesus cures a man with dropsy (Luke 14:1-6).
42. Jesus restores two blind men near Jericho (Matt. 20:29-34).
43. Jesus curses a fig tree (Matt. 21:17-22).
44. Death of Ananias and Sapphira (Acts 5:5-10).
45. Peter and John cure a lame man (Acts 3:2-11).
46. Peter and other apostles delivered from prison (Acts 5:19-23).
47. Philip carried away by the Spirit (Acts 8:39).
48. Paul heals a cripple (Acts 14:8-10).
49. Paul casts out evil spirits and cures sick (Acts 16:16-18; 19:11-12).
50. Paul raises Eutychus to life (Acts 20:9-12).

Biblical miracles are usually classified as involving:

1. *Power over nature.* On one occasion the disciples of Jesus were crossing the Sea of Galilee in a boat, when Jesus came to them walking upon the water. He also stilled a tempest that arose, calming the lake (Matt. 14:22-33).

2. *Power over disease.* An example of this most common type of miracle which Jesus performed is that of His healing of the servant of a Centurion who lived in Capernaum (Matt. 8:5-13).

3. *Power over demons.* While traveling east of the Sea of Galilee Christ met a man in whom there was an unclean spirit, or demon, which Jesus cast out (Mark 5:1-19).

4. *Power over material things.* An example of this type of miracle is found in the story of Christ's multiplying five loaves and two fishes until there was enough food to feed five

thousand men, besides the women and children (Matt. 14:13-21).

5. *Power over death.* Upon hearing of the death of His friend Lazarus, Jesus went to Bethany and, even though Lazarus had been dead four days, raised him from the dead (John 11:1-44).

History of a People

A second, radically different view of the Scriptures is that the Bible is merely the history of a people. Critics of the Bible, whether they are out-and-out atheists or merely theological liberals, describe the Bible as merely a product of man on his own. Admittedly, the men who wrote the Bible were men with insight and ability, according to this view, but they were not being directed by the Holy Spirit. The Bible, then, is a book which comes up from man's own experiences, rather than a book that comes down from God. This liberal view of modern theology holds that miracles are legends, glorified hero stories, misunderstandings, or complete fabrications.

According to this view, the miraculous crossing of the Red Sea (Exod. 14) was actually a crossing through marsh land north of the Red Sea, rather than through the sea itself. The Egyptians, following in their heavier chariots, bogged down while the Israelites went free. Similarly, the stories concerning quail and manna (Exod. 16) were both natural phenomena, rather than miraculous provisions from God. The crossing of the Jordan River (Josh. 3) was not a miracle, but merely the result of an opportune earthquake which shook sandbanks along the Jordan into the stream somewhere above the point of crossing, damming up the water long enough for the Israelites to walk through the empty stream bed. The destruction of Jericho, according to this liberal interpretation, was also by convenient earthquake (Josh. 6). Joshua's long day (Josh. 10:6-15) is explained as a misunderstanding of the later writers. The day was so unpleasant, that it just seemed to be long. Similarly, the prophets are explained away as having had no special fore-telling power. This necessitates the late-dating of some of the Old Testament books, but this is accepted seemingly without any qualms. In similar fashion, Christ's miracles are explained as merely legendary stories which grew up about a popular hero.

These naturalistic explanations of the various miracles of the Bible may seem quite plausible to some, but they become untenable when one reads the actual accounts of the miracles in the Scriptures. The eyewitness testimony does not lend itself to these liberal interpretations. The men and women who testified as to the truthfulness of these events were men and women of character and integrity, and were in possession of the normal physical senses. There is no more reason to doubt their testimony about these events than there is to doubt the testimony of others who provide the raw material out of which all history has been written.

Summary

The Christian religion, as set forth in the Bible, is so interlaced with miracles that one could hardly separate the miraculous from the rest of Christianity without destroying the whole thing. The Biblical view is that God, the Creator of the universe, set the general laws of nature in motion by which He governs the universe. Occasionally, when it serves a worthy purpose, He steps in miraculously, over-ruling some natural law or setting it aside for a time, and performs a miracle. If one believes the Bible to be the inspired Word of God, he must inevitably accept the factuality of the miracles described in the Scriptures. Only if one denies that the Bible is a book from God can he explain the miracles as natural phenomena. A "de-mythologized," or naturalistic, Bible is no Bible at all.

25

What About Miracles Today?

It is seldom, if ever, possible to *prove* that a miracle has happened. It depends upon the attitude of the person whether it can be proved or not. The doubter says simply that there has been a misunderstanding of the facts, that there has been deception, or that there are laws of nature that we do not yet comprehend. When a mind has been closed to the reasonableness or the possibility of miracles, it is difficult, if not impossible, to establish the factuality of a miracle.

The Bible's claims for miracles, we confidently believe, are reasonable. If the evidence establishing the idea that there is a God who created the universe is accepted, it is not unreasonable to believe that the same God might continue to be interested in His creation and occasionally intervene directly. It is more reasonable to believe that God would continue to be interested in that which He has created than it is to believe that He would wind it up like a clock and leave it without any further notice or concern.

The manner in which God works miracles can be illustrated by the power of the human will. As an example, man wills, and muscular force is exerted which controls or counteracts natural laws, as when he hurls a stone into the air against the law of gravitation. For a few brief moments man's will counteracts the law of gravity. To a limited degree, this suggests how the will of God supersedes the natural laws of the universe.

It is as if the creator of an elaborate model railroad, while normally operating his system from a control box, occasionally picks up an engine by hand and places it at a new location. God normally operates the universe according to His own natural laws, but occasionally when it serves a worthy purpose He steps in and causes something to happen directly, or miraculously. This was the case, for example, when King Hezekiah was given an extra fifteen years of life. It was the case when the widow's son at Nain was raised from the dead. If there is a God in heaven, who is to say that it is unreasonable to think that He would occasionally step into His own created universe and do something directly?

Characteristics of Bible Miracles

The miracles of which we read in the Bible are not irrational and non-sensical, happening in so haphazard a manner that they are utterly out of keeping with the concept of an orderly Creator. Rather, they have careful planning and purpose behind them. Notice especially these three characteristics of Biblical miracles:

1. *They exhibit the character of God and teach truths about God.* The healing miracles, about which we read throughout the New Testament gospels and the Book of Acts, are evidences of God's loving concern for His creatures. Like a human father, He responds to the needs of His children. Just as logical, but in the opposite direction, there are the punishment miracles. As an example we might refer to the miraculous death of Nadab and Abihu, (Lev. 10:1-7), who were priests of God but who rebelled against their God-given instructions and offered strange fire. As a result God caused them to be punished by death.

2. *There is an adequate occasion for them, or religious purpose.* Quite reasonably, God worked a series of spectacular miracles at the beginning of the universe. We read of these creation miracles in Genesis 1. In similar fashion, God worked a spectacular miracle at the beginning of the church on Pentecost. On that occasion He empowered the

apostles to speak in such a manner that the various people could hear in their own native tongue, thus showing His endorsement of the proceedings of that strategically important day (Acts 2). Throughout both the Old and New Testaments, we find that when God's people obeyed His commandments, they received blessings and, contrariwise, we find that when they violated His commands they were punished.

The apostle John plainly declared that the miracles of which he had written in his Gospel were to confirm the word and to produce faith. He said simply, "Many other signs therefore did Jesus in the presence of the disciples, which are not written in this book: but these are written, that ye may believe that Jesus is the Christ, the Son of God; and that believing ye may have life in his name" (John 20:30-31).

In contrast to the religious purpose which accompanied the miracles of which we read in the Scriptures, there are certain uninspired apocryphal gospels which tell of such things as Jesus making clay pigeons and turning them into live ones. Another of the stories tells about Jesus, as a child, becoming angry at other children and killing them. These are spurious writings, which can be traced back only to a period several centuries after the inspired New Testament was complete. It is interesting to observe that in this situation the inspired record itself brands these accounts as spurious. For example, the account of Christ's turning of water into wine at the marriage feast in Cana of Galilee is significant. The story ends with these words, "This beginning of his signs did Jesus in Cana of Galilee, and manifested his glory; and his disciples believed on him" (John 2:11). If this was His beginning miracle, it follows that He did not perform miracles as an angry child.

3. *They are established not by the number of witnesses, but by the character and qualifications of the witnesses.* Allow your mind to range over the entire list of the miracles of the Bible, throughout both the Old and New Testaments. Then, think of those people who testified as to the factuality of the miracles, or who accepted the

miraculous accounts at full value. You find, in the first place, that the miracles themselves were reported by sincere, capable people who gave every evidence of being men and women of absolute honesty and integrity. In the second place, you find that these miracles were believed by the finest men and women in history. The prophets of the Old Testament, including such stalwarts as Moses, Joshua, Daniel, Isaiah, and Jeremiah, the apostles of the New Testament, including the sterling characters of Peter, James, and John, and also Christ, the divine Son of God, all believed in the authenticity of the miracles of which we read in the Scriptures. We are in good company indeed when we believe in the miracles of the Bible.

Immanent or Transcendent?

In this study it is important that we focus upon the question, "Is God immanent or transcendent?" Some have contended that God is aloof from the affairs of the earth—that He is transcendent. Others have believed that He is often seen or felt in history—immanent. It is our belief that He is in constant contact with the earth, guiding events, shaping the course of history, and protecting His children. Witness the story of Joseph (Gen. 37-50), the story of Esther (Esther 1-10), the story of Paul (Acts 9-28), and many other stories throughout the Bible. This view is clearly presented in such passages as "Let every soul be in subjection to the higher powers: for there is no power but of God; and the powers that be are ordained of God" (Rom. 13:1). An even more familiar passage is from the pen of the apostle Paul in an earlier chapter of Romans: "And we know that to them that love God all things work together for good, even to them that are called according to his purpose" (Rom. 8:28).

We believe that God operates His universe by means of natural laws for the most part, but occasionally, when it serves some legitimate purpose, He steps in directly and works a miracle. C. S. Lewis has written, "All the essentials of

Hinduism would, I think, remain unimpaired if you subtracted the miraculous, and the same is almost true of Mohammedanism. But you cannot do that with Christianity. It is precisely the story of the great Miracle. A naturalistic Christianity leaves out all that is specifically Christian."[1]

Three Attitudes

There are basically three attitudes toward miracles which are held by modern man. Notice each of these carefully:

1. *Miracles have never occurred.* This is the view of the atheist, or the liberal, who says simply that none of the Biblical accounts of miraculous events are credible. This destroys much, if not all, of the Biblical picture of Christianity and also the Biblical picture of a loving Father continually concerning Himself about His children.

2. *Miracles did occur during Biblical times, but not now.* This is a denial that God empowers men "to work miracles," as He did in Biblical times. In other words, it is a denial that God enables men to work miracles as He enabled Peter, or Paul, or others of the apostles to perform miraculous acts by His power. Such passages as I Corinthians 13:8-11 give support to this idea:

> Love never faileth: but whether there be prophecies, they shall be done away; whether there be tongues, they shall cease; whether there be knowledge, it shall be done away. For we know in part, and we prophesy in part; but when that which is perfect is come, that which is in part shall be done away. When I was a child, I spake as a child, I felt as a child, I thought as a child: now that I am become a man, I have put away childish things.

While it may be difficult to define the expression "when that which is perfect is come," it seems quite legitimate to interpret it as meaning when the Lord's kingdom had been fully

---

1. *Miracles,* p. 83.

established and His gospel had been fully explained through the inspired Scriptures.

An understanding of the essential purpose behind miracles is important at this point. The primary reason for miracles, as declared in John 20:30-31, and elsewhere, is that they served to convince men of the divinity of Christ and thus to cause them to believe. The miracles were to authenticate the message of Christ and also of Christ's apostles in the minds of men. While on the earth Christ did not raise all the people who were dead, nor give sight to all of those who were blind, nor hearing to all of those who were deaf, nor health to all of those who were diseased. Rather, He performed a relatively small number of miracles in order that He might create faith. The same was true with His specially selected apostles and a few others who were empowered to work miracles. When the essential purposes for which Biblical miracles were performed no longer required them, it would seem that such miracles ceased.

The so-called modern "faith healing" miracles of our day are open to suspicion. Even the most avid enthusiasts for modern miracles do not tackle the matter of raising the dead, nor are they willing to submit to careful scrutiny by the medical profession. There are other explanations of the claimed healings which are more convincing than the demonstrations of the spectacular, showmantype religious healers of our time. Suffice it to say, that since 50 percent or more of those who go to the medical profession for help are suffering from psychosomatic illnesses, this is a large area in which faith-healers can operate. When a person who only thinks himself ill is convinced that he is no longer ill, he is not ill. In specially contrived situations, the power of suggestion works wonders, but these wonders fall far short of authentic miracles. They are a far cry from the true miracles mentioned in the Bible. *Finally, however, I would like to point out that this denial of authentic miracles worked by the agency of men, as in apostolic times, is not a denial that God in answer* to the Christian's prayer will cause certain things to happen which would not otherwise happen.

3. *Miracles still occur.* While we do not believe, for reasons just stated, that *men* are empowered to work miracles as in Biblical times, we do confidently believe that God still intervenes in the affairs of men directly, in answer to the prayers of His children. To put it another way, *God* still works miracles, as He intervenes in the normal affairs of this universe from time to time when it serves His purpose to do so.

Summary

We are convinced that it is more reasonable to believe that the Creator of the universe continues to be interested in and concerned about affairs on the earth than it is to believe that He is transcendent and aloof from the earth and man's activities. In view of the careful, purposeful manner in which the Biblical miracles are presented during the entire sweep of Biblical history, we believe that it is reasonable to conclude that they were authentic. The testimony concerning their factuality came from sources that are as dependable as any of those of ancient times on any subject. These were competent observers telling what they saw and heard.

Men of the twentieth century sometimes refer to these ancient people as being superstitious, implying that they were naive and knew little. This charge must be examined in terms of the type of miracles that these Biblical characters testify to have observed. Even though they may not have known anything about modern science, they were fully capable of knowing when a man was dead, or when he was blind, or when he was lame. They were fully capable of knowing when a dead man had been raised, or a man who had been lame for forty years was suddenly able to walk freely. In fact, their observation would be just as dependable as the observation of the most enlightened scientist of the twentieth century in these matters.

Since the primary purpose for which miracles were performed in Biblical times is no longer operative, it is reasonable to believe that miracles performed through the agency of
man, as in Bible times, no longer are to be seen on earth
today. This is not to deny, however, that God still occasionally intervenes in the affairs of men when it serves His divine
purpose to do so.

Part Six

The Divinity of Christ

> ... *for I know him whom I have believed, and I am persuaded that he is able to guard that which I have committed unto him against that day.*
>   *—The Apostle Paul*

26

The Life and Teachings of Jesus

Belief in Christ as the divine Son of God is the very center of the Christian religion. For this reason it is obviously important that consideration be given in a study of Christian evidences to the matter of His identity. There was a time some years ago when certain critics were questioning whether Jesus of Nazareth had ever lived on the earth. That time is gone. No respectable scholar now doubts that a real historic person known as Jesus of Nazareth lived, had a great influence on people, and died as a martyr. The question still remains in the minds of some as to whether this Jesus was the incarnation of God on earth, or whether He was merely a great teacher and leader of men. It is to the solution of this question that we turn.

The qualities and characteristics of the life of Jesus give evidence of His divinity:

1. *Christ was sinless.* The Scriptures pay this ultimate tribute to Jesus. The writer of Hebrews says of Him, "For we have not a high priest that cannot be touched with the feeling of our infirmities; but one that hath been in all points tempted like as we are, yet without sin" (Heb. 4:15). The apostle Peter wrote, " . . . because Christ also suffered for you, leaving you an example, that ye should follow his steps: who did no sin, neither was guile found in his mouth . . . " (I Peter 2:21-22). This quality of sinlessness is indeed impressive, in view of the many weaknesses and foibles in the lives of all others. It is an interesting exercise to think back over the life of Jesus, as revealed in the Scriptures, trying to find one

questionable act or thought or word attributed to Him. What other life can be examined with such thorough scrutiny and yet stand up under this merciless test?

Philip Schaff wrote of Him:

> In vain do we look through the entire biography of Jesus for a single stain or the slightest shadow on his moral character. There never lived a more harmless being on earth. He injured nobody, he took advantage of nobody. He never spoke an improper word, he never committed a wrong action.[1]

2. *Christ was holy, separate, apart, other, consecrated.* Not only was He sinless, by which we mean the absence of moral blemishes, but He was also holy, by which we mean that He possessed the positive qualities of spirituality. He was a model of piety and holiness. He demonstrated what He preached. His whole life and teachings are completely at variance with the idea that He made false claims concerning Himself and His divinity. Deception and the false front were condemned by Him (Matt. 23) more vigorously than any other sin. How strange it would be for Him to be living a lie, in view of the excellence of His life and the high moral and ethical message which He brought.

3. *Christ's words were the greatest words ever spoken.* Dr. Bernard Ramm writes the following concerning Christ's message:

> Statistically speaking, the Gospels are the greatest literature ever written. They are read by more people, quoted by more authors, translated into more tongues, represented in more art, set to more music, than any other book or books written by any men in any century in any land. But the words of Christ are not great on the grounds that they have such a statistical edge over anybody else's words. They are read more, quoted more, loved more, believed more, and translated more because they are the greatest words ever spoken. And where is their greatness? Their greatness lies in the pure, lucid

---

1. *The Person of Christ* (Boston: American Tract Society, 1882), p. 32-33.

spirituality in dealing clearly, definitively, and *authorita-tively* with the greatest problems that throb in the human breast; namely, Who is God? Does He love me? Does He care for me? What should I do to please Him? How does He look at my sin? How must I treat others?[2]

4. *Christ's influence on history and man is immeasurable.* Philip Schaff spoke concerning Christ's influence:

> ... this Jesus of Nazareth, without money and arms, conquered more millions than Alexander, Caesar, Mo-hammed, and Napoleon; without science and learning, he shed more light on things human and divine than all philosophers and scholars combined; without the elo-quence of schools, he spoke such words of life as were never spoken before or since, and produced effects which lie beyond the reach of orator or poet; without writing a single line, he set more pens in motion, and furnished themes for more sermons, orations, discussions, learned volumes, works of art, and songs of praise, than the whole army of great men of ancient and modern times.[3]

Dr. Ramm also speaks of the influence of Jesus:

> Whether Jesus be man or God, whether the gospels be mainly fiction or fancy, certainly a historic person named Jesus gave certain men such an impact as to be unequaled by far in the entire annals of the human race. After nearly two thousand years the impact is not at all spent, but daily there are people who have tremendous revolu-tionary experiences which they associate with Jesus Christ, be He dead or risen in heaven. The personality of Jesus is without parallel. It is unique and incomparable.[4]

5. *Christ performed supernatural acts.* Those eye-wit-nesses who wrote concerning Christ's life testified to a super-natural birth, supernatural ministrations, His possession of supernatural knowledge, and His ability to do supernatural things. Nature obeyed His command; disease was overcome

---

2. *Protestant Christian Evidences,* p. 170.
3. Schaff, pp. 29-30.
4. Ramm, p. 171.

by His word. The blind, the deaf, and the lame had their lost faculties restored. The demonic world obeyed His commands. Even the dead were brought back to life.

6. *Christ manifested the love of God.* In His life, as well as in His words, Jesus manifested the supreme example of pure, unsullied, unselfish love. He preached and practiced an unconditional love. Even in the act of dying, He prayed for forgiveness for those who were His murderers. He loved not only the great, the rich, and the talented, but also the down-trodden, the poor, and the ne'er-do-wells. No other man in history even begins to approach His life in this most vital point.

The apostle John wrote concerning God, "He that loveth not knoweth not God; for God is love" (I John 4:8). If God is love, then it would seem to follow that the one who most fully demonstrated love could claim to be His divine Son. On one occasion Jesus said, " . . . he that hath seen me hath seen the Father . . . " (John 14:9). Not only did Jesus claim to be the Son of God, but His life demonstrated His love for God and His love for man. It was Jesus who replied, when asked to name the first commandment of all, "The first is, Hear, O Israel; the Lord our God, the Lord is one: and thou shalt love the Lord thy God with all thy heart, and with all thy soul, and with all thy mind, and with all thy strength. The second is this, Thou shalt love thy neighbor as thyself. There is none other commandment greater than these" (Mark 12:29-31). His emphasis on love was preeminent.

A Beautiful Tribute

In a familiar, moving passage an unknown author has described Christ in these words:

> Here is a man who was born in an obscure village, the child of a peasant woman. He grew up in another village, and that a despised one. He worked in a carpenter shop for thirty years, and then for three years He was an itinerant preacher. He never wrote a book. He never held

an office. He never owned a home. He never had a family. He never went to college. He never put His foot inside a really big city. He never travelled, except in His infancy, more than two hundred miles from the place where He was born. He had no credentials but *himself.*

While still a young man, the tide of popular opinion turned against Him. His friends ran away. One of them betrayed Him. He was turned over to His enemies. He went through the mockery of a trial. He was nailed upon a Cross between two thieves. His executers gambled for the only piece of property He had on earth, His seamless robe. When He was dead, He was taken down from the cross and laid in a borrowed grave through the courtesy of a friend. Nineteen wide centuries have come and gone, and today Jesus is the centerpiece of the human race, and the leader of all human progress.

I am well within the mark when I say that all the armies that ever marched, all the navies that were ever built, all the parliaments that have ever sat, and all the kings that have ever ruled *put together* have not affected the life of man upon his earth like this one solitary personality.

All time dates from His birth, and it is impossible to understand or interpret the progress of human civilization in any nation on earth apart from His influence. Slowly through the ages man is coming to realize that the greatest necessity in the world is not water, iron, gold, food and clothing, or even nitrate in the soil; but rather Christ enshrined in human hearts, thoughts and motives,

Summary

Both by His life and His teachings Jesus of Nazareth demonstrated that He was unique among men. No one has ever pointed out a real flaw in His behavior, even though He lived and died under great pressure. No one has ever taught so high a system of morals and ethics. After nineteen centuries no better system has been proposed to mankind. On a more advanced level than anyone else who has lived, Jesus showed what an unconditional, unselfish, total love means. Truly He has been the central figure of all time.

27

Evidences of the Resurrection

Nothing is more crucial in the entire field of Christian evidences than the question of the divinity of Christ. Nothing is more crucial in establishing the divinity of Christ than His resurrection from the dead. If indeed He was raised from the dead, there can be no question of His divinity. The word *resurrection* in itself means a rising from the dead, and assumes that death has been experienced. Christ Himself placed great emphasis upon His resurrection, telling His disciples beforehand what would happen and predicting that He would be raised from the dead. In the minds of the apostles and other disciples nothing was more convincing of their Lord's divinity. Down through the centuries this has been the crucial evidence that Christ was no mere man. Let us, then, look at the evidence supporting the claim of resurrection.

Old Testament Evidence

In verse 10 of the sixteenth Psalm, David wrote, "For thou wilt not leave my soul to Sheol; Neither wilt thou suffer thy holy one to see corruption." Centuries later on the day of Pentecost, when the church began, the apostle Peter in his famous sermon quoted this reference from the Psalms and then added, "Brethren, I may say unto you freely of the patriarch David, that he both died and was buried, and his tomb is with us unto this day. Being therefore a prophet, and knowing that God had sworn with an oath to him, that of the fruit of his loins he would set one upon his throne; he foreseeing this spake of the resurrection of the Christ, that neither was he left unto Hades, nor did his flesh see corruption. This Jesus did God raise up, whereof we are all witnesses" (Acts 2:29-32).

Finding a prophetic quotation in the Old Testament concerning the coming of the Messiah and then finding a New Testament reference to its fulfillment is not uncommon. The reader is referred to chapter 23 of this study, where scores of Old Testament prophecies concerning the coming of Christ are mentioned along with the New Testament passages in which they were fulfilled.

New Testament Evidence

Christ anticipated His own death and resurrection, plainly declaring to His disciples not only that He should die but even the manner in which His death would be brought about. The apostle John quoted Jesus as saying, "Destroy this temple, and in three days I will raise it up. The Jews therefore said, Forty and six years was this temple in building, and wilt thou raise it up in three days? But he spake of the temple of his body. When therefore he was raised from the dead, his disciples remembered that he spake this; and they believed the Scripture, and the word which Jesus had said" (John 2:19-22). Luke quoted Jesus as saying, "The Son of man must suffer many things, and be rejected of the elders and chief priests and scribes, and be killed, and the third day be raised up" (Luke 9:22).

Matthew quoted Jesus as saying, " . . . for as Jonah was three days and three nights in the belly of the whale; so shall the Son of man be three days and three nights in the heart of the earth" (Matt. 12:40). A little later in Matthew's Gospel we read, "From that time began Jesus to show unto his disciples, that he must go unto Jerusalem, and suffer many things of the elders and chief priests and scribes, and be killed, and the third day be raised up" (Matt. 16:21). At another time Jesus was even more explicit in predicting His death: "Behold, we go up to Jerusalem; and the Son of man shall be delivered unto the chief priests and scribes; and they shall condemn him to death, and shall deliver him unto the Gentiles to mock, and to scourge, and to crucify: and the third day he shall be raised up" (Matt. 20:18-19). Later, these same writers testify to the fact that Christ's death occurred just as He had said it would.

From the remainder of the New Testament we know many additional facts. We know where, when, why, and how Christ died from the accounts in the four Gospels and in Acts. We know who got His body, under what circumstances, and where it was laid. The Gospels also concur in asserting that Christ's resurrection had the following details connected with it: (1) It took place on the first day of the week; (2) It was first discovered by the women; (3) The stone was rolled away when the women arrived; (4) Angels were present; (5) Jesus appeared to different individuals at different times, as well as to groups of individuals; and (6) He gave every evidence of being their Master of pre-crucifixion days, still possessing the power to perform the miraculous, and having a body characterized by some sort of substantiality, yet having a new set of supernatural characteristics.

The preaching of the apostles in the early church emphasized, more than any other known fact relating to Christ, His miraculous resurrection. From Peter on Pentecost through the writings of the apostle Paul and on through the writings of John in Revelation, the resurrection was given a primary place. It was the crucial evidence that Jesus was not merely a man, but the divine Son of God.

Evidence of Church History

Both ecclesiastical history and creedal history from the earliest times affirm the resurrection. It was mentioned by Clement of Rome in his *Epistle to the Corinthians,* written about A.D. 95, the earliest, datable, uninspired document of church history. It also appeared in all forms of the *Apostles' Creed* and was never debated.

The course of events of early church history was such that only the resurrection adequately explains it. The spread of the early church, the personal lives of the apostles and others, Paul's conversion, and many other known facts can be explained only by solid belief in the fact that Jesus was raised from the dead. The early Christians staked their lives upon His resurrection.

H.D.A. Major, Principal of Ripon Hall, Oxford, and editor of *The Modern Church Man,* writes:

> Had the crucifixion of Jesus ended His disciples' experience of Him, it is hard to see how the Christian Church could have come into existence. That Church was founded on faith in the Messiahship of Jesus. A crucified Messiah was no Messiah at all. He was one rejected by Judaism and accursed of God. It was the Resurrection of Jesus, as St. Paul declares in Romans 1:4, which proclaimed Him to be the Son of God with power.[1]

The Empty Tomb

One of the two most significant testimonies to the fact of Christ's resurrection is the empty tomb. The evidence pertaining to the fact that the tomb of Joseph of Arimathaea, in which the body of Jesus was placed on Friday, was empty of that body on Sunday morning, is abundant in the Gospels. The women who had carefully watched the burial of Jesus from a distance, to their utter astonishment seventy-two hours later found that the stone was rolled away and that the body was gone. They rushed back to Jerusalem and informed the unbelieving apostles. The guards also came into the city and informed the Sanhedrin, which body then concocted the story which they commanded the soldiers to repeat thereafter to explain how the tomb became empty, namely, that the body was stolen by the disciples.

Skeptics and critics have made many attempts to explain the empty tomb:

---

1. Book I, *Incidents in the Life of Jesus,* in Major, Manson, and Wright, *The Mission and Message of Jesus* (New York: E. P. Dutton and Co., 1946), p. 213.

(1) Some have charged that the body was stolen by the disciples. We would ask, "How could sleeping soldiers know? If they had really neglected their duty by sleeping, what would have been their fate? Why would the disciples have wanted to steal the body? If they had stolen it, how can we explain their future lives?"

(2) Others have charged that the body was removed by Joseph of Arimathaea. This claim dates back, however, only to a German theologian of the nineteenth century. There is no real evidence for his claim. Again we would ask, "What reason could Joseph have had for removing the body? How could he have done so with a Roman guard before the tomb? How could he have completely deceived the other disciples?"

(3) Some have argued that the women went to the wrong tomb on Sunday morning. We would ask, "How could this be possible in so small a cemetery? Did the angels also make a mistake?"

(4) The swoon theory, yet another charge of critics, holds that Jesus did not actually die, but only swooned. We would ask, "Could the people at the cross be so completely deceived? Were Roman soldiers so inept at carrying out their responsibilities of crucifixion? If Jesus did not die at this time, when did He die, and under what circumstances?"

Canon Liddon, preaching in St. Paul's in London, once said the following about the resurrection:

> It is the central sanctuary of our Christian faith. No other spot on earth says so much to the Christian faith as does the tomb of our Lord. Observe, it is the 'place where our lord *lay*.' He lies there no longer. He was not lying there when the angel addressed Mary Magdalene. With most tombs the interest consists in the fact that all that is mortal of the saint or the hero or the near relative rests beneath the stone or the sod on which we gaze."[2]

The empty tomb still stands as a convincing evidence that Jesus was raised from the dead. Those who doubt His divinity

2. Henry Parry Liddon, *Sermons. The Contemporary Pulpit Library* (New York: 1888), pp. 71-73.

have a burden of proof which they must shoulder, showing how He did die and what happened to His body, if the story of His resurrection is not true.

Testimony of the Postresurrection Appearances

During the period between His resurrection and His ascension into heaven, Christ appeared on at least ten occasions to His disciples. The record in the Scriptures is from direct eye-witness accounts of these appearances. These were unlearned and ignorant people, but they did have the usual physical senses. They had known Jesus before, and they testified that they saw Him alive after they had seen Him die on the cross. His appearances were:

(1) To certain women as they returned from the sepulchre . . . (Matt. 28:1-10).

(2) To Mary Magdalene at the sepulchre . . . (John 20:11-18: Mark 16:9-11).

(3) To the apostle Peter, before the evening of the day of the Resurrection . . . (Luke 24:34; I Cor. 15:5).

(4) To the two disciples, Cleopas and another, on the way to Emmaus . . . (Mark 16:12-13; Luke 24:13-35).

(5) To the ten apostles, Thomas being absent . . . (Mark 16:14-18; Luke 24:36-40; John 20:19-23; I Cor. 15:5).

(6) One week later, to all the eleven apostles . . . (John 20:26-28).

(7) To several of the disciples at the Sea of Galilee, while they were fishing . . . (John 21:1-23).

(8) To the apostles, and above five hundred brethren, at once, on an appointed mountain in Galilee . . . (Matt. 28:16-20; I Cor. 15:6).

(9) To James . . . (I Cor. 15:7).

(10) To the apostles at Jerusalem, immediately before the Ascension, on the Mount of Olives . . . (Mark 16:19; Luke 24:50-52; Acts 1:3-8).[3]

---

3. William Milligan, *The Resurrection of Our Lord* (London: 1881), pp. 250-251, as quoted by Wilbur M. Smith, *The Supernaturalness of Christ* (Boston: W. A. Wilde Company, 1954), p. 198.

The kind of evidence which modern science is so insistent upon in determining the reality of any object under consideration (empirical evidence) is the kind of evidence that is presented to us in the Gospels regarding the resurrection of the Lord, namely, the things that are seen with the human eye, touched with the human hand, and heard with the human ear.

Critics and unbelievers have lodged primarily two objections against the appearances of Christ after His death:

(1) *The vision hypothesis.* This is the view that Christ did not appear to His disciples in reality, but only as a vision. We would ask, "Is there ever such a thing as a vision appearing to a group or a crowd of people? Is a vision sufficient in power to change disappointed disciples into happy Christian martyrs? Why did such visions all end so suddenly, a few weeks after Christ's resurrection?"

(2) *The television theory.* This idea holds that the Lord ascended in His spirit, not (in such a theory) in His body. It then holds that Christ televised pictures of Himself to the minds of the apostles, in such a vivid way that they were actually led to believe that they had seen the risen Lord. We would ask, "Did Christ not eat with them and allow them the opportunity of feeling His side? Did they not walk with Him and talk with Him?"

If ever there was a man in the first century who knew all the arguments against the resurrection of Christ which the Sanhedrin could draw up, that man was Saul of Tarsus. Yet, in spite of all this, he came to believe that Christ had been raised from the dead by the power of God, and, believing this, he became the great apostle Paul who preached the resurrection of Christ throughout the Roman Empire.

Lord Lyndhurst, Attorney General of Great Britain and three times High Chancellor of England during the past century, wrote, "I know pretty well what evidence is; and, I tell you, such evidence as that for the Resurrection has never broken down yet."[4]

Canon Westcott added:

> Indeed taking all of the evidence together, it is not too much to say that there is no single historic event better or more variously supported than the Resurrection of Christ. Nothing but the antecedent assumption that it must be false could have suggested the idea of deficiency in the proof of it. And it has been shewn that when it is considered in its relation to the whole revelation of which it is a part, and to the conditions of the Divine action, which we have assumed, this miraculous event requires a proof in no way differing in essence from that on which the other facts with which it is associated are received as true. In a word, the circumstances under which God is said to have given a revelation to men in the Resurrection of the Lord Jesus were such as to make the special manifestation of power likely or even natural; and the evidence by which the special Revelation is supported is such as would in any ordinary matter of life be amply sufficient to determine our action and belief.[5]

Dr. Howard A. Kelly, Emeritus Professor of Gynecology Surgery at Johns Hopkins University, in his book, *A Scientific Man and the Bible,* lists the following "clear evidences" of the resurrection:

> The fact that it was utterly unexpected by the disciples and that their astonishment was great (Luke 24:4).
> It is constantly certified by the disciples who saw and companied with our Lord after his resurrection (Acts).
> By the evidences of his power over death (during his earthly life).
> By the transformation wrought in his disciples once assured of it and receiving the gift of the Holy Spirit.
> By his eating and drinking with them after rising from the dead (Luke 24:41; John 21:13; Acts 10:41).

---

4. John Singleton Copley, Lord Lyndhurst (1772-1863), as quoted by Smith, *Therefore Stand,* pp. 425, 584.

5. Brooke Foss Westcott, *The Gospel of the Resurrection,* 3rd ed. (London: Macmillan and Co., 1874), p. 136.

By all the blessed results flowing out over the world through the following centuries."[6]

Sometimes the impression is left that the greatest minds of the world reject the resurrection of Christ. The fact is, however, that some of the greatest minds of all ages, including our own scientific twentieth century, solidly believe in the resurrection of Jesus from the dead. This has been true of countless kings, presidents, and other political leaders, of great numbers of scientific men, of hosts of professional men, and, of course, of the masses who make up the rank and file of humanity.

Dr. Wilbur Smith, in his monumental book, *Therefore Stand,* wrote:

> To reject the Resurrection is to go against every law of logic which man has discovered; to reject the Resurrection is to put out the one great light that can illuminate our future; to reject the Resurrection is to involve ourselves, for the rest of life, in all kinds of efforts to explain the principles and teaching and work and influence of Jesus Christ; to deny the Resurrection of Christ is to forfeit any right to preach in a Christian pulpit, to talk to others about the blessings of following Jesus, or to kneel down at the bedside of a dying man or woman and expect to bring them any comfort.[7]

Summary

Since the resurrection of Christ occurred in the realm of history, we have sought definite, historical data to support its truthfulness. We have found the same kind of empirical evidence, through the testimony of competent eye-witnesses, that we look to for an authentic record of any ancient event. The essential facts are, as testified by these men and women of honesty and integrity, that they knew Christ personally, that they saw Him die on the cross at the hands of the

6. (Philadelphia: The Sunday School Times Company, 1925), p. 128.
7. Smith, p. 437.

Roman soldiers, that after three days the tomb was found empty, and finally that they saw Him alive in a series of personal appearances. The testimony of the empty tomb and the bodily appearances of Jesus stand without refutation.

If, as some claim, there was deception and the resurrection of Christ was a hoax, we wonder what then did become of the body of Jesus after He was killed on the cross? Why did the embarrassed Roman government not produce the body and settle the matter of Christianity for all time? Why did Christ's enemies on the Sanhedrin not produce the body and complete the matter that they had set out to accomplish, namely, the discrediting of Jesus? All that was necessary was for His enemies to produce the body and to show that truly He had been killed and remained dead. This they did not do, though they would have given any amount of money in order to have done so. One finds it hard to explain how the apostles and other disciples would give up home, family, wealth, and prestige, in order to belong to a hated sect that wore the name of a despised martyr. They had everything to lose by being Christians, nothing of worldly significance to gain. Yet, they ultimately paid with their lives in order to be true to their convictions that Jesus was the Christ, the divine Son of God—dead, buried and resurrected.

Part Seven

Situation Ethics

Essentially, Situation Ethics poses the question of who is to be the judge, God, or man?

                                    —John Sembla

28

The Case for Situation Ethics

One evening several years ago I found myself sitting at dinner across from a man whom I had just met. In the course of the conversation he said, "There are some people who believe that all religious truth was revealed nineteen hundred years ago in the Bible." Then he made it very clear that he would have no part of such an antiquated view. He believed in progressive revelation. He further elaborated his views somewhat as follows: "What was true then might not be true now. Conditions change. Through the centuries man has achieved new insights and discovered new religious truths. There is really no one body of eternal, unchanging truth. What is true in some sections of the world for some people, may not be true for other people and in other places. Truth is relative, subject to modification and change." Such views are rather widespread in our day and need serious consideration by Christians.

A teacher in a large, modern, metropolitan high school presented to her senior class, made up of some forty students, the problem of the relativity of truth. "Is truth relative, or is there a fixed body of eternal truth?" she asked them. Almost unanimously they answered that there is no one body of absolute, unchanging truth. In the essays which the students wrote, they generally agreed that in the realm of moral and ethical judgments there is no eternal right and wrong. Rather, what is right depends upon the circumstances.

During Religious Emphasis Week at a large state university I discussed with a group of twenty-five junior and senior girls the same question. Is truth relative? If one is willing to believe the more outspoken students in that particular group, there is no absolute truth. After a discussion of some length, in which I was unable to establish any one moral, ethical principle which the group would accept as true under all circumstances, one girl concluded her case, "Christ might be divine for us here in America, but not necessarily for those who live in India." To say the least, there is a very widespread view in our time that truth is relative and that situations determine what is right and what is wrong.

Situation Ethics

The most prominent exponent of "Situation Ethics" or the "New Morality" is Dr. Joseph Fletcher, author of *Situation Ethics,* published in 1966 by the Westminster Press. A representative list of situationists would include the names of Emil Brunner, Karl Barth, Dietrich Bonhoeffer, Rudolph Bultmann, H. R. Niebuhr, Joseph Sittler, James Gustafson, Paul Lehmann, Gordon Kaufman, Charles West, and Paul Tillich. Most of these men would be classified as liberals in their theology, which means that they consider the Bible to be the product of man's spiritual genius rather than a book from God.

In the foreword to his book Fletcher introduces situation ethics with this anecdote:

> A friend of mind arrived in St. Louis just as a presidential campaign was ending, and the cab driver, not being above the battle, volunteered his testimony. "I and my father and grandfather before me, and their fathers, have always been straight-ticket Republicans." "Ah" said my friend, who is himself a Republican, "I take it that means you will vote for Senator So-and-So." "No," said the driver, "there are times when a man has to push his principles aside and do the right thing." That St. Louis cabbie is this book's hero.[1]

---

1. From *Situation Ethics* by Joseph Fletcher. (Philadelphia: The Westminster Press, 1966 by W. L. Jenkins), p. 13. Used with permission.

Fletcher further states his case for situationism:

> The situationist enters into every decision-making situation fully armed with the ethical maxims of his community and its heritage, and he treats them with respect as illuminators of his problems. Just the same he is prepared in any situation to compromise them or set them aside *in the situation* if love seems better served by doing so. . . . The situationist follows a moral law or violates it according to love's need. . . . Only the commandment to love is categorically good.[2]

Situationism can also be called contextualism, occasionalism, circumstantialism, or even actualism. Its main thesis is that circumstances alter rules and principles.

Joseph Fletcher further states:

> *Christian* situation ethics has only one norm or principle or law (call it what you will) that is binding and unexceptionable, always good and right regardless of the circumstances. That is "love"—the *agapé* of the summary commandment to love God and the neighbor. Everything else without exception, all laws and rules and principles and ideals and norms, are only *contingent,* only valid *if they happen* to serve love in any situation. . . . It is necessary to insist that situation ethics is willing to make full and respectful use of principles, to be treated as maxims but not as laws or precepts.[3]

Early in his book Dr. Fletcher mentions three possible approaches to the making of moral decisions. First, there is the *legalistic approach,* with emphasis upon laws and principles which are considered to be rigidly binding. Second, there is the *situational approach,* emphasizing the principle of love alone. Third, there is the *antinomian approach,* with its chaotic unconcern for laws and principles. Dr. Fletcher claims that both the legalistic and the antinomian approaches are extremes and that neither is a satisfactory basis for the living of one's life or the guiding of society in general.

---

2. Fletcher, p. 26.
3. Fletcher, pp. 30-31.

Rather, the middle-of-the-road approach of situationalism is, according to his view, the wisest, best solution.

The case for situationism is also advanced by reference to the three Greek words which refer to the concept of love. Situation ethics is not to be guided by *eros,* or romantic physical love. Again, it is not to be guided by *philia,* or the love of friendship. Rather, it is to be guided by *agape,* or unconditional, nonreciprocal love. It is "goodwill at work in partnership with reason." Situation ethics holds that "people are at the center of concern, not things." It further holds that "people are more important than principles."

Dr. Fletcher advances six basic propositions, using them as chapter headings in his book:

1. Only one thing is intrinsically good; namely, love: nothing else at all.

2. The ruling norm of Christian decision is love: nothing else.

3. Love and justice are the same, for justice is love distributed, nothing else.

4. Love wills the neighbor's good whether we like him or not.

5. Only the end justifies the means; nothing else.

6. Love's decisions are made situationally, not prescriptively.

Examples

Dr. Fletcher, in supporting his case, tells of a German woman who was separated from her family during World War II. After the war her husband, daughter and son returned to Berlin, reestablishing the household, but she was retained in a prison camp in East Germany. Her family needed her, yet the only way she could be released from the camp was either to become critically ill or to become pregnant. After some soul-searching, she enticed a guard, became pregnant and was released to go home to her family in Berlin. Instead of resenting her "immorality" her husband and family praised her for her generous sacrifice for them. The child that was ultimately born, instead of being disliked or even hated, was loved with a special love because he had made possible the mother's return. This story was told as an example of self-sacrificing love. What this woman did was for the good of her family, and therefore, according to situation ethics, was not morally wrong, but on a higher level, ethically right.[4]

Dr. Fletcher used another example. Assuming that abortions are always wrong he set up a particular case as a challenge. A girl who had a serious mental illness was sent to a mental hospital. During her stay in the hospital, through carelessness of an attendant, a mentally deranged patient caused her to become pregnant. The child would be hopelessly abnormal, so the path of love demanded that an abortion be performed. Here, again Fletcher endeavored to take something that is normally considered to be wrong and to show that it would be right, according to situation ethics.[5]

Scriptural Support

The situationist eagerly seeks support for his views in the Scriptures themselves. Finding the story of Christ and His disciples walking through the grain fields, he immediately uses this as support for his position:

> And it came to pass, that he was going on the sabbath day through the grainfields; and his disciples began, as they went, to pluck the ears. And the Pharisees said unto him, Behold, why do they on the sabbath day that which is not lawful? And he said unto them, Did ye never read what David did, when he had need, and was hungry, he, and they that were with him? How he entered into the house of God when Abiathar was high priest, and ate the showbread, which it is not lawful to eat save for the priests, and gave also to them that were with him? And he said unto them, The sabbath was made for man, and not man for the sabbath: so that the Son of man is lord even of the sabbath (Mark 2:23-28).

4. Fletcher, pp. 164-165.
5. Fletcher, p. 37.

Thus, it would appear that both David and Christ set aside certain laws and restrictions when it seemed good to do so.

The situationist is also quick to point out certain other Scripture passages which Christians generally feel may be set aside under certain circumstances. As an example, take the requirement of church attendance, based in part, upon the statement in Hebrews 10:25, ". . . not forsaking our own assembling together, as the custom of some is, but exhorting one another; and so much the more, as ye see the day drawing nigh." Yet, Christians generally feel that when one is ill this requirement of the Scriptures can legitimately be set aside. Similarly, if one, on his way to worship on Sunday, should witness a terrible automobile accident and should see people critically injured, it would be more Christian for him to stop and aid the dying than it would be for him to go on his way to worship. Similarly, the apostle Paul's command in I Corinthians 16:2, "Upon the first day of the week let each one of you lay by him in store, as he may prosper, that no collections be made when I come," may safely be set aside when a Christian family faces sudden, heavy hospital expenses, or some other overwhelming financial emergency. For a time, their giving may be greatly reduced. Another case might be that when a neighbor's house burns, it would be the Christian thing to do to help in the emergency rather than to save one's funds for the church collection. These and other examples are sometimes advanced as cases in which generally accepted principles or commands are set aside when circumstances warrant.

The situationist also is likely to refer to certain statements by the apostle Paul which apparently endorse the basic principle of situationalism—love as the only basic law. To the Galatian Christians Paul wrote, "For the whole law is fulfilled in one word, even in this: Thou shalt love thy neighbor as thyself" (Gal. 5:14). To the Roman Christians he wrote, "Owe no man anything, save to love one another: for he that loveth his neighbor hath fulfilled the law" (Rom. 13:8). To the Corinthian Christians he wrote, "But now abideth faith, hope, love, these three; and the greatest of these is love" (I Cor. 13:13).

Summary

Situation ethics or the new morality is widely accepted in the modern world. It holds that people are more important than principles and that the only absolute standard or rule is that of *agape* (love). Everything else may be set aside when the cause of love seems to be better served by some other action. There are no absolutes. Truth is relative. Right behavior is to be determined by the circumstances in each new situation with the principle of love as the final guide. All other rules and maxims are to be used in an advisory capacity, only to illumine the situation.

Greeks are the same principles that have been used by modern man to build his mighty missiles. The laws of chemistry have not changed since the beginning of time. The combination of certain elements then brought about exactly the same results as they do today. This is true in every corner of the earth, in every laboratory, and under the guidance of specialists of every nationality. God's laws are universal. They do not change.

Truth is narrow. If you would like a simple demonstration of this fact, dial six of the seven digits in a normal telephone number correctly, then vary the seventh number just slightly. The result of this minor variation will be that you will find yourself 100 percent wrong in securing the desired person at the other end of the line. Miss just one digit ever so slightly, and you fail completely. God's truth does not allow itself to be bent or modified to suit the whims of man.

Christ placed great emphasis upon truth and the proper respect for truth. On one occasion He said, "I am the way, and the truth, and the life: No one cometh unto the Father, but by me" (John 14:6). Earlier He said, ". . . ye shall know the truth, and the truth shall make you free" (John 8:32). At another time He said, ". . . thy word is truth" (John 17:17). As we think of the situationist's views certain other Scripture verses come to mind: "There is a way which seemeth right unto a man, but the end thereof are the ways of death" (Prov. 14:12, KJV). "Heaven and earth shall pass away, but my words shall not pass away" (Matt. 24:35). "All flesh is as grass, And all the glory thereof as the flower of grass. The grass withereth, and the flower falleth: But the word of the Lord abideth forever" (I Peter 1:24-25). "Every scripture inspired of God is also profitable for teaching, for reproof, for correction, for instruction which is in righteousness: that the man of God may be complete, furnished completely unto every good work" (II Tim. 3:16-17).

God's Laws Motivated by Love

The laws and principles stated in God's Word are motivated

by and deeply involve *agape* (love). They were designed, not by an arbitrary tyrant, but by a loving Father, for the good of man. Take, for example, the Ten Commandments (Exod. 20:1-17). "Thou shalt not kill" was motivated by a respect for the sacredness of human life. "Thou shalt not steal" was motivated by a respect for the property which another man has achieved by his own hard work and self-discipline. "Thou shalt not bear false witness" was motivated by a sense of justice and fairness toward another man. "Thou shalt not commit adultery" was motivated by respect for the other marriage partner who has committed his or her life in marriage. If one will pause to look for it, I believe he will find that the ground upon which all of God's commandments are based is a love for man and a concern for his good. We feel this especially in commandments like that contained in Matthew 7:12: "All things therefore whatsoever ye would that men should do unto you, even so do ye also unto them: for this is the law and the prophets."

Notice a statement in Henry Drummond's noted sermon, "The Greatest Thing in the World":

> And you remember the profound remark which Paul makes elsewhere, "Love is the fulfilling of the law." Did you ever think what he meant by that? In those days men were working their passage to Heaven by keeping the Ten Commandments, and the hundred and ten other commandments which they had manufactured out of them. Christ said, I will show you a more simple way. If you do one thing, you will do these hundred and ten things, without ever thinking about them. If you love, you will unconsciously fulfill the whole law. And you can readily see for yourselves how that must be so. Take any of the commandments. "Thou shalt have no other gods before Me." If a man love God, you will not require to tell him that. Love is the fulfilling of that law. "Take not His name in vain." Would he ever dream of taking His name in vain if he loved Him? "Remember the Sabbath day to keep it holy." Would he not be too glad to have one day in seven to dedicate more exclusively to the object of his

affection? Love would fulfill all these laws regarding God.
And so, if he loved Man, he would never think of telling
him to honour his father and mother. He could not do
anything else. It would be preposterous to tell him not to
kill. You could only insult him if you suggested that he
should not steal—how could he steal from those he loved?
It would be superfluous to beg him not to bear false
witness against his neighbor. If he loved him it would be
the last thing he would do. And you would never dream
of urging him not to covet what his neighbors had. He
would rather they possessed it than himself. In this way
"Love is the fulfilling of the law." It is the rule for
fulfilling all rules, the new commandment for keeping all
the old commandments, Christ's one secret of the Christian life.[1]

God's laws simply spell out in careful detail what the principle of love requires. Without these guidelines most men would be unable to apply the basic principle of love in all situations where they find themselves. Especially, when he is
under great emotional stress would he find it difficult to
know what love requires, without these specific statements of
principles and commands from God.

The whole thing can be put in proper perspective by a
little story. Three little girls were talking one day about the
restrictions which their mothers placed upon them. The first
little girl said, "My mother lets me cross the street." The
second little girl, not to be outdone, responded, "That's
nothing. My mother lets me play anywhere in the neighborhood that I want to play." The third little girl, after a few
moments' hesitation, timidly added her part to the conversation, "My mother doesn't let me cross the street. She doesn't
let me play anywhere in the neighborhood that I want to
play. . . . My mother loves me." God places certain restrictions upon us because He knows what is for our good and
because He loves us.

---

1. *The Greatest Thing in the World, and 21 other Addresses* (London: Collins,
1953), pp. 48-49.

Man Does Not Know

Man does not always know what *agape* (love) requires in every situation. After all, he never has lived before. He never has been over the road before. His perspective is quite limited. He sometimes thinks that he knows what is right, yet later finds that he was very wrong. Man is a finite creature of imperfect powers and perceptions. It was the prophet Isaiah who wrote, speaking for God, "For my thoughts are not your thoughts, neither are your ways my ways, saith Jehovah. For as the heavens are higher than the earth, so are my ways higher than your ways, and my thoughts than your thoughts" (Isa. 55:8). Man is not capable of knowing what is right or wrong, good or bad, in every situation, but God is. *Through obeying God's laws we serve love, because there is no real conflict between the laws of God and the principle of absolute love.*

This whole point can be conveyed in a simple experience which many have shared. For a number of years my family and I, while living in California, spent repeated vacation periods in Yosemite National Park, one of the most beautiful places on earth. We often drove to the top of one of the mountain rims which overlook the Yosemite valley, a spot known as Observation Point. There, we had an opportunity to look down upon the valley some three thousand feet directly below us. From this vantage point we could see what we could not see from the valley floor. For example, a beautifully paved road winding through the pine trees takes a turn and ends at the park dump, where the garbage from the various hotels and camps is deposited each night. Another beautiful road leads around a curve and then branches off to the tool shed where the maintenance vehicles and tools are kept. Down on the valley floor each of these appealing side-roads has a sign saying simply "Dead End." Looking down from above, we knew why. Other valley roads, appearing very much as the ones mentioned above, lead through their windings eventually to beautiful Mirror Lake, or to

Happy Isles, or to Vernal Falls, or to some other scenic spot. It was only from the rim above the valley that we could see the wisdom of the markings on the roads below. Only from that perspective could we see that some roads lead to beauty and happiness while other roads lead to ugliness and disappointment. From His vantage point, as Creator and Sustainer of the universe, God knows those roads that lead to ruin and despair and marks them with prohibitions. He also knows those roads that lead to success and happiness, and guides men along them.

Man Is Not Mature Enough

A common objection to situation ethics is that it calls for more critical intelligence, more factual information, and more self-starting commitment to righteousness than most people can bring to bear. Situationism ignores the reality of human sin or egocentricity, and fails to appreciate the finitude of human reason. Situation ethics presumes more ability to know the facts and weigh them than most people can muster. Man is not always mature enough to do what *agape* (love) requires in every situation. In the midst of the battle of life, man often cannot objectively and coolly decide what love requires. It is also easy to mix *agape* with *eros*. Under pressure, man often obeys the laws he likes and disobeys the laws he does not like. This leads to confusion and chaos.

The whole crux of the matter is, "Who is to be the judge?" Is God, who created the universe, including man, and who knows all of the intricacies of life, better suited to decide what is right behavior in any given situation? Or, is man, who himself is involved in the complexities of life, both as a sinner and through his own emotional involvement, better able to make right decisions about ethical behavior? We believe that God is better able to know how man ought to behave, for God alone has the grasp of the entire situation and the objectivity to know what is right and what is wrong.

Questions Answered

What about those times when David, or Christ, seemed to set aside God's principles? What about those occasions when the Christian sets aside God's commandment to attend worship or to give of his financial means? The answer is quite simple. *Only when a higher principle of God is involved is it legitimate to set aside some lesser commandment.* While David and his men did eat the showbread which was normally unlawful for men to eat, it was when they had been driven out of the city of Jerusalem because of the jealous anger of King Saul. Their physical survival was more important than the keeping of the normal law restricting the showbread to the priests. Similarly, Christ and His disciples had the right to eat a few handfuls of grain as they passed through the fields on the sabbath day, because their physical well-being was more important than the keeping of the minutest sabbath day restriction which the over-zealous Pharisees had placed upon men. Similarly, when one is ill it is a higher law, the respect for life itself, that excuses him from attending worship.

This view is borne out in the Scriptures themselves. For example, the apostle Paul commanded in Romans 13:1, "Let every soul be in subjection to the higher powers: for there is no power but of God; and the powers that be are ordained of God." This obviously means obedience to the laws of the land. However, we find that there are occasions when it is legitimate to disobey the laws of the land. They are rare, but an example is found in the case when the rulers commanded the apostles "not to speak at all nor teach in the name of Jesus" (Acts 4:18). They had a prior, higher command from Christ Himself, "Go ye into all the world, and preach the gospel to the whole creation" (Mark 16:15). As a result of this higher command, the apostles continued to preach in the name of Christ and were then re-arrested. It was at this point that Peter and the other apostles said, "We must obey God rather than men" (Acts 5:29). Only when there is some

29

The Case Against Situation Ethics

While situation ethics has an appealing first sound, as one visualizes it in actual practice he soon comes to see that it is too simple. Man, being what he is, cannot make it work. Man tends to respect those laws which he wants to respect and to reject those which he wants to reject. This would lead to anarchy and ultimately to the total breakdown of civilization. This whole theory places too high an estimate upon man. Situation ethics does have an appealing first sound, but careful examination proves it is inadequate. It is far better in theory than it is in practice. There is another side to the story.

Absolute Truth

Upon careful observation one discovers that there is such a thing as absolute truth. There are many situations in which truth is not relative at all. Take for example, God's natural laws which surround us in the universe. God has two kinds of laws: the natural, physical laws that are so apparent in our universe, and the moral, spiritual laws which He reveals to us in His inspired Word. We can learn much about His moral laws by studying His physical laws. For example, God's physical laws are universal, applying to all people in all places and for all times. The law of gravity is just as real today as it was in the day of the Medes and the Persians. It applies just as much in Africa or Asia as it does in America. No person on earth is exempt from its pull. Similarly, the principles of mathematics which were known and respected by the ancient

243

higher law of God or principle of God do we have the right to set aside some specific requirement.

What about the examples given in Joseph Fletcher's *Situation Ethics?* Was the action taken by the German woman in a prison camp moral or immoral? What about abortion, as in the case of the girl who was mistreated in a mental hospital; *First of all, any system of morals and ethics which must resort to unusual, isolated and unlikely situations for support demonstrates its own weakness in so doing.* How often is a person likely to find himself in the situation of the German woman in the prison camp? How often is the pregnancy situation of the mental hospital illustration likely to appear in a normal life? *What mankind needs is not a system of ethics for those rare, hypothetical situations just mentioned, but rather a system that can be used day in and day out and even hundreds of times every day and used not by just a few but by all people.* Then, too, before one can say that the German woman's act was morally good, he would need to know what effect it had on the prison guard and his family, upon the woman herself and on the future behavior of her children. In this light, situation ethics must be judged as an impractical, idealistic system that requires unusual knowledge and unusual willpower on the part of those who would follow it. For the masses of men and for all the circumstances of life it seems indeed an unacceptable system.

Summary

Contrary to the view of the situationists, the Christian who believes the Bible to be the inspired Word of God believes that the rules and regulations which one finds in the Bible are framed by God for the express purpose of helping man to know what love requires in every situation of life. Rather than leaving the matter to man himself, so deeply and so emotionally involved in life, God lays down rules as to what loving behavior is in each situation.

At first sound, situation ethics has an appeal, but as one

looks more deeply into this philosophy of life, he realizes that it will not work. Man is neither intelligent enough nor morally sensitive enough to decide in every situation what loving behavior is. Christ's way of life, so beautifully demonstrated in His life and in the lives of the early Christians, offers man his best hope for a peaceful world, a happy life, and a future home in heaven.

Part Eight

Conclusion

The acknowledgement of God in Christ,
accepted by thy reason, solves for thee
all the problems in this world and out of
it.

—Robert Browning

30

The Will to Believe

William James, the noted pioneer psychologist and philosopher of Harvard University, delivered a lecture which he called "The Will to Believe" to the Philosophical Clubs of Yale and Brown Universities. This later became the title of a book of his essays. As he indicated in the beginning of his message, it was "an essay in justification *of* faith, a defence of our right to adopt a believing attitude in religious matters. . . ."[1] The lecture is of great value to us today since it deals with the question of whether it is reasonable to believe, in the religious sense.

In his introductory material Dr. James defined certain terms. The word *hypothesis* means "anything that may be proposed to our belief." There may be *living* options, in which a person can see some possibility of truth. Options may be *forced*, meaning that the person must make a decision one way or the other, or *avoidable*, meaning that a person need make no decision whatever. Options may be *momentous*, vitally important to one's life, or *trivial*, of no real significance at all. The matter of religious faith, rather obviously, is a *living, forced,* and *momentous* option.[2]

At this point in his lecture Dr. James introduced a famous paragraph from Blaise Pascal's writings:

1. William James, *The Will to Believe* (New York: Longmans, Green and Co., 1937), p. 1.
2. James, pp. 2-3.

You must either believe or not believe that God is—
which will you do? Your human reason cannot say. A
game is going on between you and the nature of things
which at the day of judgment will bring out either heads
or tails. Weigh what your gains and your losses would be
if you should stake all you have on heads, or God's
existence: if you win in such case, you gain eternal
beatitude; if you lose, you lose nothing at all. If there
were an infinity of chances, and only one for God in this
wager, still you ought to stake your all on God; for
though you surely risk a finite loss by this procedure, any
finite loss is reasonable, even a certain one is reasonable,
if there is but the possibility of infinite gain. . . . Why
should you not? At bottom, what have you to lose?[3]

After some discussion of the comments of Pascal, William
James made his conclusion with these words:

Pascal's argument . . . seems a regular clincher, and is
the last stroke needed to make our faith . . . complete.
The state of things is evidently far from simple; and pure
insight and logic, whatever they might do ideally, are not
the only things that really do produce our creeds.[4]

Dr. James continued:

The thesis I defend is, briefly stated, this: *Our passional nature* [the part of man involved in feelings and will]
*not only lawfully may, but must, decide an option be-
tween propositions, whenever it is a genuine option that
cannot by its nature be decided on intellectual grounds;
for to say, under such circumstances, "Do not decide, but
leave the question open," is itself a passional decision,—
just like deciding yes or no,—and is attended with the
same risk of losing the truth.*[5]

Later on in his lecture, he made this observation:

Objective evidence and certitude are doubtless very
fine ideals to play with, but where on this moonlit and
dream-visited planet are they found?[6]

---

3. James, pp. 5-6.
4. James, p. 11.
5. James, p. 11.
6. James, p. 14.

Developing his thought further he added:

> . . . we must go on experiencing and thinking over our experience, for only thus can our opinions grow more true; but to hold any one of them—I absolutely do not care which—as if it never could be reinterpretable or corrigible, I believe to be a tremendously mistaken attitude. . . .[7]

After pointing out that good minds have been on both sides of almost every nameable question, or hypothesis, Dr. James made this statement:

> . . . there is indeed nothing which some one has not thought absolutely true, while his neighbor deemed it absolutely false. . . .[8]

Next, attention was turned to the question of two ways of looking at our duty in the matter of opinion, or judgment. One of those ways is, "We must know the truth," while the other is, "We must avoid error." At first, these seem to be saying the same thing from slightly different points of view, but upon examination one discovers that they are actually two different approaches to decision making. Taking the latter first, the mind is primarily dedicated to the thesis that one should "keep [his] mind in suspense forever, rather than by closing it on insufficient evidence incur the awful risk of believing lies."[9] Such a view holds that it is "Better [to] go without belief forever than believe a lie!" On the other hand, the other approach finds a person thinking ". . . that the risk of being in error is a very small matter when compared with the blessings of real knowledge. . . ." Then, "Our errors are surely not such awfully solemn things. In a world where we are so certain to incur them in spite of all our caution, a certain lightness of heart seems healthier than this excessive nervousness on their behalf."[10]

7. James, p. 14.
8. James, p. 16.
9. James, p. 18.
10. James, p. 19.

Next, Dr. James said that "not only as a matter of fact do we find our passional nature [feelings and will] influencing us in our opinions, but that there are some options between opinions in which this influence must be regarded both as an inevitable and as a lawful determinant of our choice."[11] He asked still later, "Are there not somewhere forced options in our speculative questions, and can we . . . always wait with impunity till the coercive evidence shall have arrived?"[12] In this discussion he added, "Moral scepticism can no more be refuted or proved by logic than intellectual scepticism can. When we stick to it that there *is* truth (be it of either kind), we do so with our whole nature, and resolve to stand or fall by the results. The sceptic with his whole nature adopts the doubting attitude; but which of us is the wiser, Omniscience only knows."[13]

At another time Dr. James spoke of scepticism:

> Scepticism, then, is not avoidance of option; it is option of a certain particular kind of risk. *Better risk loss of truth than chance of error,*—that is your faith-vetoer's exact position. He is actively playing his stake as much as the believer is; he is backing the field against the religious hypothesis, just as the believer is backing the religious hypothesis against the field. To preach scepticism to us as a duty until "sufficient evidence" for religion be found, is tantamount therefore to telling us, when in presence of the religious hypothesis, that to yield to our fear of its being error is wiser and better than to yield to our hope that it may be true.[14]

A little later he stated the area in which this thesis is particularly applicable: ". . . the freedom to believe can only cover living options which the intellect of the individual cannot by itself resolve; and living options never seem absurdities to him who has them to consider."[15] Then he added,

---

11. James, p. 19.
12. James, p. 22.
13. James, p. 23.
14. James, pp. 26-27.
15. James, p. 29.

"Indeed we *may* wait if we will . . . but if we do so, we do so at our peril as much as if we believed. In either case we *act,* taking our lives in our hands."[16]

Finally, Dr. James concluded his essay with a quotation from Fitz James Stephen:

> What do you think of yourself? What do you think of the world? . . . These are questions with which all men must deal as it seems good to them. . . . In all important transactions of life we have to take a leap in the dark. . . . If we decide to leave the riddles unanswered, that is a choice; if we waver in our answer, that, too, is a choice: but whatever choice we make, we make it at our peril. If a man chooses to turn his back altogether on God and the future, no one can prevent him; no one can show beyond reasonable doubt that he is mistaken. If a man thinks otherwise and acts as he thinks, I do not see that any one can prove that *he* is mistaken. Each must act as he thinks best; and if he is wrong, so much the worse for him. We stand on a mountain pass in the midst of whirling snow and blinding mist, through which we get glimpses now and then of paths which may be deceptive. If we stand still we shall be frozen to death. If we take the wrong road we shall be dashed to pieces. We do not certainly know whether there is any right one. What must we do? "Be strong and of good courage." Act for the best, hope for the best, and take what comes. . . . If death ends all, we cannot meet death better.[17]

Summary

In those situations where it is not possible to know complete and absolute truth—in those situations which involve faith—it is better to take the path of hope than the path of fear. After all, what have we to lose? When we add to this the impressive evidence reviewed in this book—touching all phases of the Christian view of life—faith and hope are more reasonable choices than doubt and despair.

---

16. James, p. 30.
17. James, p. 31, quoting from Fitz James Stephen, *Liberty, Equality, Fraternity,* 2nd ed. (London, 1874), p. 353.

Appendix I

The Providence of God

I firmly believe in the providence of God. I believe that God determines both the events of our lives and the events of the world. I further believe that God controls and guides the events of our world in such a way as to bless His children. That is what I mean when I say I believe in divine providence. This idea was expressed years ago in the Constitutional Convention of our country when Benjamin Franklin, the noted statesman, rose and addressed General George Washington who was presiding, saying, "I have lived, Sir, a long time, and the longer I live, the more convincing proofs I see of this truth—*that God governs in the affairs of men....* If a sparrow cannot fall to the ground unseen by him, was it probable an empire could arise without his aid?"[1] Franklin was saying what many of us have said and felt: God governs in the affairs of men.

Is It Reasonable?

If someone should ask, "Why do you believe that God shapes the events of our world to conform to the needs of Christians?" I would answer, "I believe it because it is reasonable." We live in a world which was created primarily for man. Man was created as God's crowning work, and the animal, plant, and material worlds were placed under his dominion. God formed this world to meet the needs of man.

1. Catherine Drinke Bowen, *Miracle at Philadelphia* (Boston: Little, Brown & Co., 1966), p. 126.

Is it reasonable to suppose that the God who created such a magnificent creature as man, and formed such a remarkable world for man, would then go off and forget man's needs?

If we human fathers are mindful of the needs of our youngsters, working continually for them and constantly concerned for their welfare, is it not infinitely more likely that the God who made the world would continue to be concerned about those who are His children? The agreeableness of our world, the congeniality of nature, adds up to what I believe is an unanswerable argument that God continues to be concerned about man's problems.

Testimony of the Scriptures

Someone might ask, "But are there other reasons?" I would say, "Yes, the second reason why I believe that God does govern in the affairs of men is that He says so in His inspired book." Turn for a moment to the eighth chapter of Romans, to that familiar and wonderful passage in which the apostle Paul, guided by inspiration, says, "And we know that to them that love God all things work together for good, even to them that are called according to his purpose" (Rom. 8:28).

In this brief passage, there are at least four factors which stand out. First, the apostle says, "we know." There is no hesitance or uncertainty. It is knowledge with him. It is not mere belief, a mere possibility, but rather an absolute certainty. The second thing that stands out is that he includes "all things," not a few of the events of our lives, but all the events of our lives. The third element is that they "work together for good." In spite of the trials, tribulations, and afflictions that may come upon man, God will never allow final, absolute evil to overtake him. While there may be valleys along the road of life, ultimately there will be a mountain peak. The ultimate and final good of man is announced in this great promise. All things work together for good. The fourth thing in this passage is that the promise is only for those who are God's children. It is limited to lovers of God. "And we know that to them that love God all things work together for good." There is no promise in this passage to those who are not Christians, to those who are not conformed to the will of God.

The Power of God's Love

Later in the same chapter of Romans, we find a further assurance that the love of God will be manifested in the lives of His children:

> What then shall we say to these things? If God is for us, who is against us? He that spared not his own Son, but delivered him up for us all, how shall he not also with him freely give us all things? Who shall lay anything to the charge of God's elect? It is God that justifieth; who is he that condemneth? It is Christ Jesus that died, yea rather, that was raised from the dead, who is at the right hand of God, who also maketh intercession for us. Who shall separate us from the love of Christ? shall tribulation, or anguish, or persecution, or famine, or nakedness, or peril, or sword? . . . Nay, in all these things we are more than conquerors through him that loved us. For I am persuaded, that neither death, nor life, nor angels, nor principalities, nor things present, nor things to come, nor powers, nor height, nor depth, nor any other creature, shall be able to separate us from the love of God, which is in Christ Jesus our Lord (Rom. 8:31-35, 37-39).

It is obvious that the apostle Paul believed that God was taking care of His children. He believed that nothing on this earth could separate us from the love, the concern, and the care of God.

There is another passage, one which the apostle Paul wrote to the Corinthians, which says the same thing:

> For our light affliction, which is for the moment, worketh for us more and more exceedingly an eternal weight of glory; while we look not at the things which are seen, but at the things which are not seen: for the things which are seen are temporal; but the things which are not seen are eternal" (II Cor. 4:17-18).

The light afflictions of our world do sometimes burden us down, but then we stop to realize whose we are and where we are going, and we take a new lease on life. We are on our way to an eternal home in heaven, and God will help us get there.

Measuring By the Wrong Standard

Man sometimes falters, however, in his belief that God governs in the affairs of men. He looks at the world about him and sees a righteous man, who is genuinely devoted to God, suffer. It may be through illness, or the loss of money, or the loss of friends, or in some other way. Then, he sees another man, who isn't righteous at all, prosper. So he says, "How can I believe that God blesses the good? Why, there is evidence that He doesn't. How can I believe in divine providence when the evidence of my eyes and my ears is against it?"

The answer lies in the fact that man is deluded into thinking that this world is his home. He is deluded into thinking that the material things of this world—the riches, the honors, the pleasures—are the main things of life. When he thinks along these lines, he has simply chosen the wrong standard by which to measure. It is the wrong yardstick. *Man's primary purpose in existence is to honor and glorify God and to become as God-like as it is humanly possible to become. Now this being so, everything that takes him away from God is evil, and everything that brings him toward God is good.*

When we have accepted this standard, we can see the events of our world in a different light. It is quite possible that the riches, the honors, and the pleasures of this world are actually hindrances rather than helps. It is quite conceivable that poverty is better than riches. At least Jesus said, "A man's life consisteth not in the abundance of the things which he possesseth" (Luke 12:15). The Lord also said, "It is easier for a camel to go through a needle's eye, than for a rich man to enter into the kingdom of God" (Matt. 19:24). All too often the material things of our world blind us to the spiritual things and thus become curses instead of blessings, not just for time, but for eternity. Riches, honors, and pleasures are not necessarily evil; they can also be blessings. It depends on our attitude toward them; it depends on how we use them. Do they draw us closer to God or pry us away from God?

It is quite possible that the frowns of the world are better than its honors. It is quite possible that illness is better than health. "Oh, that's unthinkable," you say. But remember, our primary concern in living is to honor and glorify God. The man who spends some time on his back in a hospital room often sees things in a clearer light than he ever saw them while he was going through life without a care. I do not say that when we become sick we are to rejoice, but I do believe that if we accept illness in the proper manner, it can be a blessing.

The Value of Suffering

It is by suffering that we overcome. A man who has no sorrow in his life is immature. It is through suffering that we develop physical stamina. It is through suffering that we learn to overcome the lust of the flesh, the lust of the eye, and the pride of life. Things that looked so glamorous before, after a period of crisis in which we come face to face with the real issues of life, look like tinsel and glitter, mere baubles on a Christmas tree.

There is a passage in the Letter to the Hebrews in which God tells us that He allows us to suffer because of His love for us:

> For whom the Lord loveth he chasteneth, And scourgeth every son whom he receiveth. It is for chastening that ye endure; God dealeth with you as with sons; for what son is there whom his father chasteneth not? But if ye are without chastening, whereof all have been

made partakers, then are ye bastards, and not sons. Furthermore, we had the fathers of our flesh to chasten us, and we gave them reverence: shall we not much rather be in subjection unto the Father of spirits, and live? For they indeed for a few days chastened us as seemed good to them; but he for our profit, that we may be partakers of his holiness. All chastening seemeth for the present to be not joyous but grievous; yet afterward it yieldeth peaceable fruit unto them that have been exercised thereby, even the fruit of righteousness. (Heb. 12:6-11).

David made a similar testimony:

It is good for me that I have been afflicted; That I may learn thy statutes" (Ps. 119:71).

I remember standing at a bedside some time ago and looking down on a man who had had two or possibly three years snatched out of the prime of his life by tuberculosis. He had the faith to say, "Well, in the long run it is a blessing. It has enabled me to study the Scriptures more than I would have ever been able to study them in any other way." Then he added, "I have memorized many passages that I would never have known except for this illness." David said, "It is good for me that I have been afflicted." God does govern in the affairs of men, and when He allows something to come my way or your way which is difficult to bear, it is because He loves us. He is, by that means, enabling us to grow stronger that we may some day spend eternity with Him.

Examples of Providence in the Bible

Many years ago, before the turn of the century, J. W. McGarvey preached two great sermons on divine providence. The first concerned Joseph of the Old Testament. Near the end of that sermon, after telling of the life of Joseph in detail, he made this summary:

So then, this long story is told as an illustration of the providence of God, by which He can bring about His purposes. . . . The man who studies the story of Joseph and does not see this in it, has failed to see one of its great purposes. And what is true in bringing about this result in the family of Jacob, may be true—I venture to say, it is true—in regard to every family of any importance in this world; and it extends down to the modes by which God overrules our own acts, both good and bad, and those of our friends, and brings us out at the end of our lives shaped and molded as He desires we shall be.[2]

In the evening of that same day, after he had told the story of Esther in detail, he added these comments:

A few days ago I stood in the great fair at Chicago, before a weaving machine—a wonder. There were coming out beneath the shuttles bands of silk about as wide as my hand, and perhaps a foot long, four or five coming out at one time at different parts of the loom, woven with the most beautiful figures in divers colors. One of them was "Home, Sweet Home," the words woven by that machine, and above the words was the music. There was woven at the top a beautiful cottage, trees in the yard, bee-gums, and children at play, and down below the words and music, a lone man sat, with his face resting on his hand, thinking about that distant home. All coming out of that machine. The shuttles were flying, threads were twisting and dodging about, the machine was rattling, and no human hand on it, yet there the song, the pictures, the music, were coming out. Did they come out by accident? By an accidental combination of circumstances? I could not, to save my life, tell how it was done, but I saw a pattern hanging up at one side with many holes through it, and I was told that the pattern was ruling the work of that intricate machinery, and leading to that result. I was bound to believe it. Now you could make me believe that this beautiful piece of work came out of the loom by accident, and without any man directing and planning it, just as easily as you can make me believe that this chain of circumstances, of facts, bringing about, in accordance with God's faithful promises, the deliverance of His people, was accomplished

2. *Sermons* (Louisville, Ky.: Guide Printing & Publishing Company, 1894), pp. 221-222.

without Him. God was there, my brethren. And just as little can I believe that all those intricate circumstances in my life and yours, which shape and mould and direct and guide us, which take us when we are crude and wicked men, and mould and shape us and grow us up until we are ripe and ready to be gathered into the eternal harvest— that all this is human, or all blind force, or accident, and that there is no hand of God in it.[3]

God does govern in the affairs of men.

An Interesting Illustration

C. S. Lewis, Fellow of Magdalene College, Oxford University in England, in his challenging book, *Miracles,* tells in the final chapter of the favorable weather at Dunkirk, which enabled a surprisingly large number of British and Canadian soldiers to be evacuated from the beaches before the Germans could capture them. He indicated that he agreed with the many people who considered the weather to be "providential," and then he gave his own illustration of how the providence of God works.

To him it is like the way a novelist works out the happenings in his book, only on a much greater scale. But let him say it:

Suppose I am writing a novel. I have the following problems on my hands: (1) Old Mr. A. has got to be dead before Chapter 15. (2) And he'd better die suddenly because I have to prevent him from altering his will. (3) His daughter (my heroine) has got to be kept out of London for three chapters at least. (4) My hero has somehow got to recover the heroine's good opinion which he lost in Chapter 7. (5) That young prig B. who has to improve before the end of the book, needs a bad moral shock to take the conceit out of him. (6) We haven't decided on B's job yet; but the whole development of his character will involve giving him a job and showing him actually at work. How on earth am I to get

---

3. McGarvey, pp. 245-246.

in all these six things? . . . I have it. What about a railway accident? Old A. can be killed in it, and that settles him. In fact the accident can occur while he is actually going up to London to see his solicitor with the very purpose of getting his will altered. What more natural than that his daughter should run up with him? We'll have her slightly injured in the accident: that'll prevent her reaching London for as many chapters as we need. And the hero can be on the same train. He can behave with great coolness and heroism during the accident—probably he'll rescue the heroine from a burning carriage. That settles my fourth point. And the young prig B? We'll make him the signalman whose negligence caused the accident. That gives him his moral shock and also links him up with the main plot. In fact, once we have thought of the railway accident, that single event will solve six apparently separate problems.[4]

Immediately he apologized for the imperfections of the illustration, then added that the example does "suggest how Divine ingenuity could so contrive the physical 'plot' of the universe as to provide a 'providential' answer to the needs of innumerable creatures."[5]

Man's Only Primary Concern

You and I, if we will, can fit into God's plan and thereby be blessed. If we fight against His will, we have no hope of blessing. So, when all of the evidence is in, there is just one thing that we need to be concerned about. We need not be concerned about food, nor clothing, nor shelter, for remember the words of Jesus, "Be not anxious for your life, what ye shall eat, or what ye shall drink; nor yet for your body, what ye shall put on. Is not the life more than the food, and the body than the raiment?" (Matt. 6:25). It is not for temporal things we need to be concerned. Our chief concern must be that we be counted children of God. That's the only real concern in life—that we be among those who are lovers

---

4. Lewis, p. 210.
5. Lewis, p. 211.

of God. Jesus said, "If ye love me, ye will keep my commandments" (John 14:15). A few moments later, He said again, "He that hath my commandments, and keepeth them, he it is that loveth me: and he that loveth me shall be loved of my Father, and I will love him, and will manifest myself unto him" (John 14:21). If we love God and conform to His commands, we have the promise of His love and care. James said, "Be ye doers of the word, and not hearers only, deluding your own selves" (James 1:22).

We live in God's world. God shapes the events of this world to suit His divine, eternal plan. If you and I are wise, we will fit into that plan as an evidence of our love and respect for God. We have His promise that He will take care of us in this world and in the next world which has no end.

Appendix II

The Goodness of God
and the Problem of Evil

Did God wind up the world like a clock and then go off and leave it to run down? Is He even aware of what is going on in the world today? Does He guide the affairs of men? More important, at least to me, is He aware of me and what is happening in my life? Does He care? Is there any way to reach out and make contact with God? Does He hear my prayers? These are some of the questions that men are asking today about God. Likely, all of us at one time or another have asked some of these questions. When life becomes hard, when our problems seem insurmountable, inevitably we will ask questions like these.

The answer to all these questions is that God does continue to concern Himself with our world. He created it; He sustains it. Most meaningful of all, He is deeply concerned about every person who lives—young or old, rich or poor, great or small. In the long ago Jesus said, "Are not five sparrows sold for two pence? and not one of them is forgotten in the sight of God. But the very hairs of your head are all numbered. Fear not; ye are of more value than many sparrows" (Luke 12:6-7). Jesus was saying simply that if God is concerned about the relatively unimportant sparrow, He must be deeply concerned about man.

The familiar words of John Greenleaf Whittier, in his poem, "The Eternal Goodness," bear repetition:

I know not what the future hath
Of marvel or surprise,
Assured alone that life and death
His mercy underlies.

. . . .

I know not where his islands lift
Their fronded palms in air;
I only know I cannot drift
Beyond his love and care.

A Drift Toward Humanism

In recent years there has been a strong drift toward humanism, which emphasizes man's reliance upon himself, with absolutely no consideration given to God. Far back in the fifteenth century, a movement began which credits man's achievements solely to his own aptitudes, skills, and expertise. Known as *humanism,* this system denies that any source of either assistance or restraint, higher than man himself, even exists. The humanist denies the very existence of anything divine. Man is a genius, and that is all there is. Harvey Cox, in his widely read book, *The Secular City,* defends the modern God-less trend in urban living. In his book there is the sentence, "There is no reason that man must believe the ethical standards he lives by came down from heaven. . . ."[1]

How different it is with the writers of the Scriptures. Just the opposite view was expressed by David when he said, "Jehovah is my light and my salvation; Whom shall I fear? Jehovah is the strength of my life; Of whom shall I be afraid?" (Ps. 27:1). I also remember the stirring words of the apostle Paul when he said, ". . . for I know him whom I have believed, and I am persuaded that he is able to guard that which I have committed unto him against that day" (II Tim. 1:12).

When man sees the evidence that is all about him he cannot but be impressed with the overwhelming proof that

---

1. *The Secular City: Secularization and Urbanization in Theological Perspective.* rev. ed. (New York: Macmillan, 1966), p. 35.

there really is a God. Our universe is too remarkably made not to have come from the mind of a great designer and creator. However, there are problems. There are questions for which man does not have answers. Most of these have to do with relatively unimportant matters, but a few are of major significance.

One of the most difficult is the question "How could a God of infinite goodness create a world with so much evil in it?" Many intelligent people are deeply disturbed by the evil in our world and cannot understand how God allows such evil to exist. They speak of sickness and suffering which are known wherever men live. They are impressed with the problem of death itself. Man's inhumanity to man, as seen in war, is also mentioned. Similarly, they speak of man's misuse of other men and even the subjugation of whole races of men. The universality and ugliness of sin are also pointed out. Then, too, and perhaps most difficult of all to deal with, there are earthquakes, tornadoes, hurricanes, tidal waves, and other violent, destructive acts of nature.

Two Premises

As we face this heavy objection to our Christian faith, I would point out two preliminary considerations. *First, man's knowledge is limited.* Just as a child cannot possibly understand the adult world, so man does not have the perspective to understand fully the nature of God and the makeup of the universe. Man's "line of sight" is often limited and his conclusions are often inaccurate. This, if we are honest, all of us must admit from our own experiences. As Solomon said it in the Proverbs, "There is a way which seemeth right unto a man, But the end thereof are the ways of death" (Prov. 14:12). Man is often mistaken.

Most of us are aware that when one sits down to read a page of Hebrew he begins at the right side of the page and reads across to the left, just the reverse of the way we read English. Often life needs to be read backward. There are many times when we cannot possibly understand a situation in life until we have heard the rest of the story. For example, in Genesis the story of Joseph was utterly unintelligible until the story was complete. This boy could not possibly have understood why his brothers sold him into bondage and why his father did not buy him back from the slave traders—that is, until the rest of the story unfolded and he could comprehend the purpose of it all. Reading backward, every step of his life showed a beautiful plan.

For a more modern example, I would refer to a young girl who was engaged to a man a few years older than she. As the wedding approached, he broke the engagement and in doing so broke her heart. For a time she was bitter and felt that there could not be any justice or goodness in a world where she was so shamefully treated. Later, however, she found *the man* and in that marriage achieved a higher happiness than she had dreamed possible before. She no longer had any problem about the goodness of God, but was thankful that she had not entered into the earlier less-promising marriage.

The second important premise is that man's conception of what is good is often mistaken. The pleasure-pain view of existence is shallow and incomplete. Yet, almost all mankind considers a thing good if it gives pleasure and a thing bad if it causes pain. The *summum bonum* is interpreted as happiness. Every story must end, "A good time was had by all . . . And they lived happily ever after."

This is indeed a shallow, incomplete view of life. We human beings are not the center of the universe and God is not our private lackey or servant. To evaluate everything as good or bad in terms of whether it gives us pleasure or pain is certainly self-centered. There is greater good than pleasure and greater evil than pain. Man does not exist primarily to be happy. Man, the creature, exists in order to glorify God the Creator.

Underlying Principles

Now let us come to the real explanation of why there is

evil in the world. We suggest four great, basic, underlying principles of our universe. Note each one carefully. Note that in order for each one to be present there are certain attendant circumstances which could not in the very nature of reality be avoided.

The first of these underlying principles is the regularity of law. We find it stated in the Scriptures when we read, "In the beginning God created the heavens and the earth" (Gen. 1:1). As that opening chapter of the opening book of the Bible unfolds we read that the various kinds of plants and of animals brought forth "after their kind." Other evidences of an ordered system of natural laws are also set forth. In Genesis 8:22, as a further example, we read, "While the earth remaineth, seedtime and harvest, and cold and heat, and summer and winter, and day and night shall not cease." God planned the universe so that it would be run by a system of natural laws, and by these laws everything functions. Without these laws life would be impossible. A world of chance would be chaotic.

It is precisely because of the universal laws of nature that storms occasionally occur. God's plan of causing the sun to evaporate the oceans, of winds to carry the moisture in the form of clouds over the mainland, and of atmospheric conditions which cause rain creates the possibility of floods. As waters flow down the mountains and through the valleys, as the streams carry the torrents away, it is inevitable that occasionally there will be whirlpools with attendant danger to human life. The winds that normally purify the atmosphere occasionally cause a tornado.

Gravity can be cruel, when someone falls from a height and is crushed in the fall; but without gravity it would not be possible for the normal activities of life to go on. Similarly, fire is destructive on occasion, but without fire it would not be possible to cook man's food, nor to provide power for many of life's activities. Sunshine and rain are great blessings, though occasionally the sun causes droughts and the rain causes floods. It is necessary to look at the total picture. If we look at all of nature we find that it is very good indeed. The occasionally destructive aspects of nature are so few in comparison with its blessings that the verdict must be solidly in favor of God's system.

Secondly, there is the freedom of man's will. When God chose to make man He paid him great honor by giving him freedom of will and making him a creature of choice. Man is no robot or automaton, but a creature of free will. In this crucially important act God did two things. He lifted man above the realm of the animals and above all inanimate objects on earth, giving him a dignity and an importance that are unique. At the same time God made it possible for man to choose evil as well as good. There was no other way. If man was to have freedom of will, it was inevitable that he might choose evil as well as good. Man's misuse of his freedom has brought untold suffering to humanity.

In spite of the charges of some, God is not responsible for much or even most of man's sufferings because they come from man's own unfortunate choices. As an example, we might mention a woman who married a tyrannical husband and then blamed God for her unhappy state. Actually, however, God did not cause her to marry this particular man. That was her own decision and her suffering was a result of her wrong choice. In a similar manner, when a drunken driver veers across the center line of the highway and causes a collision that takes the lives of several people, this is not God's act. It is a result of man's sin against his fellowman. There is no possession which man has that is more important than his ability to make choices, yet there is no element of his nature which has been so costly. When God made man with the capability of reaching the stars, inevitably there was connected with it the possibility of plumbing the depths.

The third underlying principle of our universe is the value of imperfect conditions. The problems, imperfections and challenges which our world contains give us opportunities for growth and development which would otherwise be impossible. Sorrow and suffering help us to develop traits which fit us for eternity. A teenage boy does not develop his muscles by lying in a hammock in the shade in the summertime and eating ice cream. Rather, he develops his muscles by the hard labor involved in mowing a lawn, constructing a house or plowing a field. The imperfections of our world serve a purpose in allowing us to grow and develop into mature responsible beings in a way which would otherwise not be possible.

The fourth underlying principle is the interdependence on human life. It was the apostle Paul who said, in Romans 14:7, "None of us liveth to himself, and none dieth to himself." Much of man's suffering results from the actions of other people, people of the past as well as the present. The misdeeds of our ancestors continue to plague us and our misdeeds will inevitably be a burden for our children. But to avoid this it would be necessary for each one of us to live in an airtight compartment. Only in this way could we avoid the interconnections of life and thereby avoid the results of the misdeeds of others.

Yet, I am convinced that our greatest blessings come from the love which we give to others and the love which we receive from others. Without this interconnectedness, life would be barren and largely meaningless. The avoidance of all contact with other human beings might save us some suffering, but it would cost us the greatest joys and pleasures of life.

The Real Nature of God

, E.?

A. D. Wilder Smith, a highly respected medical doctor on the staff of the University of Illinois Medical School in Chicago, has recently written a very remarkable book, *Man's Origin, Man's Destiny*. In this recent publication he touches upon the problem of pain and suffering:

> The solution to the problem of pain . . . is to be found just where solutions to many other problems of life are to be found, namely, in the character and life of Christ. Let

us ask ourselves first of all what Christ's attitude to pain
and death was. This we can rapidly ascertain if we look at
his most prominent activity in life, which was, of course,
going about healing and doing good. This means simply
that he made it his job to reverse pain and death. He
raised Lazarus and Jairus' daughter from the dead. But
this attitude was not confined to Christ, for his apostles
referred to death as the last *enemy.* Christ referred to
people with certain sicknesses as being bound by the
devil. If Jesus Christ considered himself to be God's Son
(there is no doubt that he did), he considered that he was
doing God's works in reversing pain and death, as enemies
of God. He said he was doing what he saw the Father
doing. Thus Christ reflected God's attitude when he went
about reversing pain and death and their consequences. . . .

On reading the Bible more carefully, there is really
never any question of reconciling God with pain, suffering and death as though he were the real author of
them—even though he may use pain for his purposes. If
Christ gives any indication at all of God's attitude to pain
and death, then God is the great reverser and enemy of
pain and death. . .[2]

Conclusion

There are questions for which we have only partial answers. However, there are also certainties upon which we can
depend. Nothing is more certain than God's love. Similarly,
the evidence of God's goodness is overwhelming. God's way
is the best way. It is the most reasonable way. Ultimately, it
is the only way.

There is one thing more, a very important one. Even
though God cannot take away the evil that is inherent in the
world, He does promise that if we love Him He will see us
through. It was the apostle Paul in writing to the Romans
who assured us, "And we know that to them that love God
all things work together for good, even to them that are
called according to his purpose" (Rom. 8:28). This does not

---

2. A. E. Wilder Smith, pp. 210-211.

say that all things are good, but that if we are lovers of God He will see that all things work together for our ultimate good.

It is in a similar vein, I think, that Paul wrote to the Corinthians, "There hath no temptation taken you but such as man can bear: but God is faithful, who will not suffer you to be tempted above that ye are able; but will with the temptation make also the way of escape, that ye may be able to endure it" (I Cor. 10:13). There is no ultimate tragedy that can happen to a Christian. It is for these reasons that we believe in the goodness of God, in spite of the evil that is sometimes so distressing and so painful in our world. When one sees all of life and understands the reasons behind life's suffering, I believe he will agree with the judgment which God Himself declared in the Genesis story of creation, "And God saw everything that he had made, and behold, it was very good" (Gen. 1:31).

Bibliography

American Scientific Affiliation. *Modern Science and Christian Faith.* Chicago: Scripture Press, 1950.

Bales, James D. *Atheism's Faith and Fruits.* Boston: W. A. Wilde, 1951.

———. *Miracles or Mirages?* Austin, Texas: Firm Foundation Publishing House, 1956.

———. *Roots of Unbelief.* Rosemead, Calif.: Old Paths Book Club, 1948.

——— and Teller, Woolsey. *The Existence of God: A Debate.* Old Paths Book Club, 1948.

Campbell, Alexander and Robert Owen. *The Evidences of Christianity, a Debate.* Nashville, Tenn.: Gospel Advocate Company, 1946.

Clark, Robert E. D. *Darwin: Before and After.* Grand Rapids: International Publications, 1958.

Clark, Robert T. and James D. Bales. *Why Scientists Accept Evolution.* Grand Rapids: Baker Book House, 1966.

Cox, Harvey. *The Situation Ethics Debate.* Philadelphia: Westminster Press, 1968.

Creation Research Society, *Biology, A Search for Order in Complexity.* Grand Rapids: Zondervan Publishing House, 1970.

Darwin, Charles. *The Origin of Species,* Intro. W. R. Thomson. London: Dent, 1967.

Davidheiser, Bolton. *Evolution and Christian Faith.* Grand Rapids: Baker Book House, 1968.

Davis, Willard O. *Evolution and Revelation.* Austin: Firm Foundation Publishing House, 1968.

Davis, William H. *Philosophy of Religion.* Abilene, Texas: Biblical Research Press, 1969.

Dehoff, George. *Why We Believe the Bible.* Murfreesboro, Tenn.: Dehoff Publications, 1940.

Dewar, Douglas. *The Transformist Illusion.* Murfreesboro: Dehoff Publications, 1957.

Elam, E. A., ed. *The Bible Versus Theories of Evolution.* Nashville: Gospel Advocate Co., 1925.

Everest, Harvey W. *The Divine Demonstration.* St. Louis, Mo.: Christian Publishing Co., 1884.

Fletcher, Joseph. *Situation Ethics, The New Morality.* Philadelphia: Westminster Press, 1966.

Freud, Sigmund. *The Future of An Illusion,* trans. W. D. Robson-Scott. New York: Liveright Publishing Corp., 1953.

Gerstner, John H. *Reasons for Faith.* New York: Harper and Row [1960].

Henry, Carl F. H., ed. *Revelation and the Bible.* Grand Rapids: Baker Book House, 1958.

Hughes, Philip Edgcumbe. *Christianity and the Problem of Origins.* Philadelphia: Presbyterian and Reformed Publishing Company, 1967.

James, William. *The Will to Believe.* New York: Longman's, Green and Co., 1937.

Jauncey, James H. *Why We Believe.* Cincinnati, Ohio: Standard Publishing Co., 1969.

Kenny, Anthony. *Aquinas, A Collection of Critical Essays.* Garden City, N.Y.: Anchor Books, 1969.

Keyser, Leander. *A System of Christian Evidence.* 10th ed. rev. Burlington, Iowa: Lutheran Literary Board, 1953.

Klotz, John W. *Genes, Genesis, and Evolution.* St. Louis: Concordia Publishing House, 1965.

Lewis, C. S. *Mere Christianity.* New York: Macmillan, 1955.

––––. *Miracles.* New York: Macmillan, 1947.

Linton, Irwin H. *A Lawyer Examines the Bible.* Grand Rapids: Baker Book House, 1943.

Lunn, Arnold. *The Revolt Against Reason.*

Maatman, Russell W. *The Bible, Natural Science and Evolution.* Grand Rapids: Baker Book House, 1970.

MacKinnon, D. M., and others. *Objections to Christian Belief.* Philadelphia: J. B. Lippincott, 1964.

McGarvey, J. W. *Evidences of Christianity.* Cincinnati: Standard Publishing Co., 1886.

McMillen, S. I., M.D. *None of These Diseases.* Westwood, N.J.: Fleming H. Revell, [1963].

Meldau, Fred John. *Why We Believe in Creation Not in Evolution.* Denver: Christian Victory Publishing Co., 1967.

Mixter, Russell L., ed. *Evolution and Christian Thought Today.* Grand Rapids: Wm. B. Eerdmans Publishing Co., 1959.

Monser, J. W. *An Encyclopedia on the Evidences.* Nashville: Gospel Advocate Company, 1961.

Monsma, John C. *Behind the Dim Unknown.* New York: G. P. Putnam's Sons, 1966.

––––, ed. *The Evidence of God in an Expanding Universe.* New York: G. P. Putnam's Sons, 1958.

––––, ed. *Science and Religion.* New York: G. P. Putnam's Sons, 1962.

Moody, Paul Amos. *Introduction to Evolution,* 3rd ed. New York: Harper & Row, Publishers, 1970.

Morris, Henry M. *The Bible and Modern Science.* Chicago: Moody Press, 1956.

––––. *Biblical Cosmology and Modern Science.* Grand Rapids: Baker Book House, 1970.

––––. *Evolution and the Modern Christian.* Grand Rapids: Baker Book House, 1967.

––––. *Studies in the Bible and Science.* Grand Rapids: Baker Book House, 1966.

––––. *The Twilight of Evolution.* Grand Rapids: Baker Book House, 1964.

–––– and others. *A Symposium on Creation.* Grand Rapids: Baker Book House, 1968.

–––– and John C. Whitcomb, Jr. *The Genesis Flood.* Grand Rapids: Baker Book House, 1965.

Morrison, A. Cressy. *Man Does Not Stand Alone.* New York: Fleming H. Revell, 1944.

see p. 9c >

Nelson, Byron C. *The Deluge Story in Stone*. Minneapolis: Bethany Fellowship, Inc., 1968.

Orr, James. *The Bible Under Trial*. New York: A. C. Armstrong, 1907.

———. *Revelation and Inspiration*. Grand Rapids: Baker Book House, 1969.

Paley, William. *A View of the Evidences of Christianity*. Murfreesboro: Dehoff Publications, 1952.

Patten, Donald W. and others. *A Symposium on Creation II*. Grand Rapids: Baker Book House, 1970.

Ramm, Bernard. *The Christian View of Science and Scripture*. Grand Rapids: Wm. B. Eerdmans Publishing Co., 1955.

———. *Protestant Christian Evidences*. Chicago: Moody Press, 1957.

———. *Special Revelation and the Word of God*. Grand Rapids: Wm. B. Eerdmans Publishing Co., 1961.

Rehwinkel, Alfred M. *The Flood*. St. Louis: Concordia Publishing House, 1951.

Sears, Jack Wood. *Conflict and Harmony in Science and the Bible*. Grand Rapids: Baker Book House, 1969.

Shute, Evan. *Flaws in the Theory of Evolution*. Nutley, New Jersey: Craig Press, 1966.

Simpson, George Gaylord. *The Meaning of Evolution: A Study of the History of Life and of Its Significance for Man*. New Haven: Yale University Press, 1961.

Smith, A. E. Wilder. *Man's Origin, Man's Destiny*. Wheaton, Ill.: Shaw Publishers, 1961.

Smith, Wilbur M. *The Supernaturalness of Christ: Can We Still Believe In It?* Grand Rapids: Baker Book House, 1964.

———. *Therefore Stand*. Grand Rapids: Baker Book House, 1945.

Stonehouse, N. B. and Paul Woolley, eds. *The Infallible Word*. Grand Rapids: Wm. B. Eerdmans Publishing Co., 1946.

Thomas, J. D. *The Doctrine of Evolution*. Abilene: Biblical Research Press, 1961.

———. *Facts and Faith*. Vol. I of the series, *Reason, Science and Faith*. Abilene: Biblical Research Press, 1965.

———. *The Present Status of the Doctrine of Organic Evolution, Christian Faith in the Modern World. A.C.C. Lectures, 1960*. Abilene: Students Exchange, 1960. / missing R.A.Torrey

Trout, Virgil R. *Christian Evidences*. Austin: R. B. Sweet Co., 1963.

Ward, Rita Rhodes. *In the Beginning*. Grand Rapids: Baker Book House, 1965.

Warfield, Benjamin B. *The Inspiration and Authority of the Bible*. Philadelphia: Presbyterian and Reformed Publishing House, 1948.

Wolthuis, Enno. *Science, God and You*. Grand Rapids: Baker Book House, 1963.

Wood, Nathan R. *The Secret of the Universe, "God, Man and Matter."* Grand Rapids: Wm. B. Eerdmans Publishing Co., 1966.

Zimmerman, Paul A. *Darwin, Evolution, and Creation*. St. Louis: Concordia Publishing House, 1959.

Organizations

The American Scientific Affiliation, H. Harold Hartzler, Exec. Sec., 324½ South Second Street, Mankato, Minnesota 56001.

Bible-Science Association, Inc., Walter Lang, Exec. Sec., Box 1016, Caldwell, Idaho 83605.

Christian Research Institute, Walter R. Martin, Director, 116 Surrey Drive, Wayne, New Jersey 07470.

Creation Research Society, Wilbert H. Rusch, Exec. Sec., 2717 Cranbrook Road, Ann Arbor, Michigan 48104.

Evolution Protest Movement, A. G. Tilney, Exec. Sec., "Santhia", Stoke, Hayling Island, Hants, England.

International Christian Crusade, Inc., Gwen Smith, Exec. Sec., 205 Yonge St., Room 31, Toronto 1, Ontario, Canada.